W9-AEH-216

The Enabling Garden

SB
457.4
.H36
R68
1994

Rothert, Gene.

The enabling garden.

$13.95

DATE			

KVCC KALAMAZOO WITHDRAWN

BAKER & TAYLOR

SB
457.4
.H3C
R68
1994

The Enabling Garden
A Guide To Lifelong Gardening

Gene Rothert, HTR

Illustrated by
Laurie Noffs

TAYLOR PUBLISHING COMPANY
Dallas, Texas

WITHDRAWN

NOV 1 7 1997

To Cathy, for all her love and understanding

Design by *Deborah Jackson-Jones*
Landscape architecture by Jeff Sloot, ASLA

Copyright © 1994 Eugene A. Rothert Jr.

All rights reserved.

No part of this book may be reproduced in any form by any means without written permission from the publisher.

Published by Taylor Publishing Company
            1550 West Mockingbird Lane
            Dallas, Texas 75235

Library of Congress Cataloging-in-Publication Data

Rothert, Gene.
      The enabling garden : a guide to lifelong gardening / Gene Rothert.
            p.   cm.
      Includes bibliographical references and index.
      ISBN 0-87833-847-0
            1. Gardening for the physically handicapped.   2. Gardening for the
aged.   I. Title.
      SB457.4.H36R68   1994
      635'.087—dc20   93–41968
                                                                CIP

Printed in the United States of America

10 9 8 7 6 5 4 3 2 1

Contents

Acknowledgments

I make no bones about it. This book would not have been possible but for the many hundreds of people I have encountered throughout my life.

I am extremely grateful to the Chicago Botanic Garden, and, in particular, to Betty Bergstrom, former director of development, who provided me an opportunity sixteen years ago, fresh out of college and fresh out of rehabilitation after a spinal cord injury that requires that I use a wheelchair. This was at a time when people with disabilities were rare in the workplace.

I thank my parents, Mary and Gene, for their guidance and support, which prepared me well for life after leaving the nest.

My loving wife, Cathy, who is a professional physical therapist, was essential to the information in Chapter Two. Beyond this, she provided understanding and support through my many hours locked in a home office.

Jeff Sloot, ASLA, of Architerra, Inc., helped me immensely in the design chapter with both manuscript review and his professional drawings. Jeff is one of those rare people who willingly share their expertise with others.

Thanks also to my supervisor, Kris S. Jarantoski, Deputy Director of the Chicago Botanic Garden, for his support and, I'm sure, a certain amount of patience as this book neared completion. Special thanks go to Joan Hammer, who interpreted my alien script and tolerated my inevitable revisions. I could not have done it without her. Thanks as well to Kate Jerome, Plant Information Specialist, for her helpful manuscript review.

I want to recognize the support of my friends at the American Horticultural Therapy Association, not only for their direct contributions to this book and their dedicated efforts to encourage the use of horticultural therapy, but also for the inspiration they have been to my career.

Another individual whom I met very early in my career, who was and is a great influence both professionally and personally, is Joan Shoemaker, HTM. Her writings helped me establish a personal philosophy about horticultural therapy. Later, as she struggled with illness, she was the embodiment of "don't quit."

Lastly and most importantly, I want to thank the many hundreds of gardeners who have overcome barriers to gardening, for without their inspiration, ingenuity, and willingness to share their ideas, the concept of enabling gardening and this book may not have even gotten to the idea stage.

I must also pay a final tribute to Max Huekler, Mary O'Neal, and Florence Quirnbach. I met these dear friends on my third day of work at the Chicago Botanic Garden in June 1978. They were volunteers who helped maintain the Learning Garden for the Disabled. They truly inspired me both at a fragile point in my life and later as aging took its inevitable toll on them. They were and are forever vital, cheerful, and grateful for every minute of life—never complaining and never saying a negative word. The few hours a week in our garden were extremely important to them. Mary passed away at 103 and Max at 89, but Florence at 88, God love her, is still in the garden every Thursday morning. They're the ones that truly understood and extolled the values of gardening that no one should miss.

Preface

Opportunity can be a funny thing. I was sitting in my office at the Chicago Botanic Garden in May 1991 up to my neck in spring—the busiest season in horticulture—when the phone rang. It was public television's "The Victory Garden." They wanted to do a segment on barrier-free gardening at our Learning Garden for the Disabled, a public garden exhibit adapted for people with disabilities and older adults.

The call resulted from contacts I originally made in 1987 with the host of the show at that time, Bob Thomson, where we discussed the need to cover the subject of barrier-free gardening. Lo and behold, in early June 1991 producer Russell Morash, host Jim Wilson, and the very professional crew of what I considered the best gardening program on television showed up to film the story. Essentially, I had five minutes to tell the story that gardening is possible for everyone.

The program aired in late July 1991, and the message must have struck a chord because we were immediately inundated with hundreds of requests for information on what I began to call "enabling" garden techniques and tools. We pulled together a basic packet of information and sent it to anyone who asked. Things quieted down after a while, but when the segment was rerun we again received many letters asking for help.

It was strongly apparent that there are many gardeners who have or face mobility impairments who want to continue gardening. I knew that the information we sent could get someone started, but neither the five minutes on "The Victory Garden" nor our modest information packet provided all that needed to be said. Creating a barrier-free garden is a very individualized thing. Considering myself neither a writer and definitely not a television personality, the idea for a "Barrier-Free Gardening Guide" surfaced as a goal of the Chicago Botanic Garden's Horticultural Therapy Services Program *if* a donor or grant could be secured to fund both a writer and printing costs. Unfortunately, this and many other good ideas stay at this stage in the not-for-profit sector due to lack of funding.

Then out of the blue the phone rang again in September 1992. It was my soon-to-be editor, Holly McGuire, proposing that I write the product you have in your hands after seeing me on "The Victory Garden." I was thrilled, then immediately terrified because I was not a writer but knew enough about the craft of writing to have a great respect for writers—both for their hard work and for the difficulties of getting work. I had also just been elected President of the American Horticultural Therapy Association, which added another level of responsibility to my life.

So I said I would think about it and get back to them. In the meantime, with some very considered procrastination, I began to put together an outline for the project, determined that the book would not ruin my marriage or interfere with my other commitments. I finally realized, however, that my very astute editor had provided the "kick in the pants" I needed to do something about the opportunity to share with you how to garden for a lifetime.

Introduction

*"Enable: Create
an Opportunity to Do"*

The Enabling Garden is an area where people of all ages and abilities can participate in gardening. It goes beyond basic architectural access to become a safe, comfortable place that creates the encouraging opportunity for all people to garden. Appropriately designed, the Enabling Garden eliminates any physical barrier to gardening. For those of us who are avid gardeners, the worst thing that can happen is to have to stop. We know the peace we find in the garden, the many outlets for creativity, the exercise, and the reward of the perfect blossom or the first harvest of vine-ripened tomatoes. With the information in this book, anyone should be able to garden at some level for as long as they wish.

Statistics illustrate that gardening is one of the top two or three leisure activities for Americans over 55. American society is aging, and while age in itself is not a disability by any means, let's face it: At some point our physical stamina begins to decrease, and some activity-limiting diseases may set in. Yet age need not be a barrier in the garden.

This book is also written for those of you among the approximately 42 million Americans with some temporary or permanent physical disability. For you, *The Enabling Garden* will either permit you to continue gardening or introduce a new hobby you had never considered because of mobility impairment. If you use a wheelchair, have difficulty balancing, lack hand strength, or find traditional gardening physically too challenging, this book will help reduce or eliminate obstacles by adapting the garden to your abilities. We will also adapt *you* through enabling tools and equipment.

This book is directed to those people with disabilities and older adults who live at home. Some of the measurements, design techniques, and construction material selections recommended here may not be appropriate in a public setting, where local building codes may dictate the width of sidewalks, for example, or the slope of a curb cut or ramp. While you need to follow some codes even for most permanent private structures, you will still have greater leeway because you are building the garden to *your* customized needs on *your* property. Your needs are unique.

I am not a carpenter or architect or construction expert; hence, this book is not about construction. Also, techniques and building codes vary in different parts of the country. This book provides only basic construction ideas. For further detail, consult trade professionals or the many speciality books on garden construction and woodworking. Most of the suggested garden structures are fairly easy to construct and, if you and your helpers are reasonably good do-it-yourselfers, can be accomplished with minimal tools.

Gardening from a wheelchair or with other mobility restrictions presents its challenges, but these are easily accommodated with adaptations in techniques and equipment. Once you thoroughly evaluate your available time, overall mobility and strength, endurance, your unique height and reach limits, and what you plan to accomplish in the garden, you can create the garden layout and the equipment needed. This book will help you adapt *the garden* area to eliminate barriers to access. Finally, there's information that will help you consider plant choices from Enabling Garden perspectives.

I can relate to the mobility challenges of people with disabilities and some older adults because I am a 39-year-old wheelchair user myself, following a spinal cord injury 16 years ago. I am also a horticulturist by profession and have gained a great deal of experience working with special gardeners in gardening projects at hospitals, nursing homes, and other agencies as a horticultural therapist (HTR).

This is one of the few books on gardening that is going to tell you very little about growing plants. This book is written for gardeners with perhaps a lifetime of experience working the soil, but who are getting a touch of arthritis, can't see as well as before, or have a heart condition that limits activity. This book will help anyone make better choices about gardening activities that are appropriate and safe and how to go about them.

The information and resources here are, by necessity, fairly generalized because of the tremendous variability in people and their abilities. Some people who use wheelchairs have the great arm endurance and strength to participate in long-distance racing (not me!). Others require electric motors to move about. Most older adults would certainly not fit the term *disabled,* but many have difficulty getting up and down from the ground, walking, or bending over. To accommodate different specific needs requires very different strategies. Therefore, this book will help you evaluate and select the best garden components, tools, and plants to create your own Enabling Garden.

A great many of my experiences in barrier-free or enabling gardens have come while working with people with disabilities and older adults as a horticultural therapist at the Chicago Botanic Garden in Glencoe, Illinois, a northern suburb of Chicago. Early in my career at the Botanic Garden, I was fortunate to be responsible for its Learning Garden for the Disabled, at the time one of the few public exhibits of barrier-free gardening techniques in the country. The garden is designed to provide access to the gardening experience and its many benefits to all people, no matter what their physical abilities. The garden was the perfect place to try different construction materials, structures, tools, equipment, techniques, and plants. With the many wonderful people who have gardened there over the years, we all learned together how to continue gardening by doing it. The hundreds of shared experiences have helped me gather many enabling ideas. Much of what we learned is in this book.

A greater sensitivity to our aging society and the large minority of people with disabilities has focused the efforts of product designers on tools and other equipment that promote easier and more independent

living. Better design also has many applications to the garden, such as in the many horticultural therapy programs that serve people with disabilities and older adults. Many of these programs rely on enabling gardens for outdoor activities.

Of late, thankfully, there is a greater emphasis on home care or deinstitutionalizing people to live or recover at home. It is for the many millions of us who live at home who want to—and should—continue to garden that this book is written.

Most gardeners learn from experience and sharing information with one another. *The Enabling Garden* brings together the experience of hundreds of older and disabled gardeners with that of horticultural therapists, specially trained in the medical and psychological benefits of gardening and how to use horticulture in treatment programs. Their primary goal is to help people of all physical and mental abilities maintain or regain independence over their lives.

My next best teacher has been my own yard, where I have had to adapt my garden to be barrier-free. I have a half-acre lot with a basic one-story, three-bedroom ranch with a two-car attached garage. Here I quickly found I was spoiled by my experiences at the Chicago Botanic Garden, where the funding and staff support was there to do the "perfect" Enabling Garden. At home, the limits of budgets and physical help for construction shed a new light on the concept. I do not have the funds to build large raised beds or lay paving in every location I wanted to garden. I cannot afford to install automatic irrigation systems to make watering effortless. I had to think up more economical means to make my garden as enabling for me as possible. I will share these ideas I came up with or discovered from others throughout this book as well.

The ingenious tips and techniques in the boxes throughout have been provided by older or fellow gardeners with disabilities, who from their own experiences have adapted themselves or their gardens in very special ways. Other ideas have been provided by my friends and colleagues who are horticultural therapists, who interact with special gardeners who themselves have passed along some of their favorite ideas.

✿   ✿   ✿

A word about terminology: There is an almost continuous debate about what vocabulary to use when referring to people with disabilities or older adults. In the old days terms like crippled, spastic, lame, idiot, and other equally degrading terms were readily accepted labels.

Personally, as a person with a disability, I find it very interesting that most of this debate is among people without disabilities. Oh well, that's another story.

First, I feel all labels distract from the fact that first and foremost we are people. All people differ in their abilities, whether they are physical or intellectual. These abilities change from the day we are born until the day we die. In my case, using a literal definition, I do not have the ability to walk unassisted. Not having the *ability* to walk, see, or hear is a *disability*, pure and simple. Being a wheelchair user (rather than "bound" or "confined"), I encounter *handicaps* when stairs, narrow paths, or steep ramps limit my access to places. In other words, the environment may be handicapping based on the individual's degree of mobility. The term *older adult* seems to have emerged as the preferred term, as opposed to senior citizen *or* the elderly. This term, again, simply states the literal facts. This is the term I use in this book.

❂   ❂   ❂

One of the major goals of anyone with a disability or an older adult is to maintain independence in daily living for as long as possible. This book is about independence—independence in the garden. Many of the ideas you learn for making life easier in general also apply in the garden. For example, levers are easier to use than knobs on doors and should also be used on gates and water spigots. I hope that after reading this book you can apply many of the techniques for gardening to be a lifelong activity, no matter what your age or degree of mobility. After all, "old gardeners never die—they just spade away."

What Gardening Gives You

All of us who garden, whether tending a few pots of colorful geraniums on a weathered balcony railing or raising enough homegrown vegetables to share with neighbors, have a deep and special understanding of the almost magical effect the garden has upon us. During the growing season the first thing I do when I get home from the office is check out the garden. What's coming up? Let's pull a few weeds. What's new in bloom? Are those color combinations I tried working? Did the deer have my phlox for breakfast again? For those ten to fifteen minutes, I'm in another world. I relax; it's as invigorating as a quick nap.

In addition to relieving stress, gardening offers many natural avenues for exercise and is a great way to burn calories. Although most gardeners strive to make gardening as easy as possible, it is common knowledge that moderate exercise is good for you. With appropriate medical supervision, you can plan your garden to provide almost any degree of physical challenge. Most joints and major muscle groups of your body can be worked through their full ranges of motion during the almost limitless range of gardening activities. As someone who uses a wheelchair, I work in the garden as one of my major sources of exercise. So I challenge myself to turn over my own planting beds in the spring, edge beds, prune, and so on. Because I enjoy collecting and caring for plants and being outdoors, I can work an hour or two and not notice it. Any time I can get exercise and not feel the "pain," that's *my* kind of exercise! Strength, balance, eye-hand coordination, range of motion, and endurance can all be challenged in the garden to just about any degree that you want—or not at all as the case may be.

Besides exercise for the body, the wide field of horticulture offers many challenges for the mind: To design the perfect border, collect and study in depth a particular group of plants, track down that rare exotic, or practice the art of pruning—all vary from the simple to the complex, with as many opinions as there are people. As far as I am concerned, horticulture is one of the most creative pursuits there is. Just about anything goes, and doing it your way is perfectly okay.

Why are plants, gardens, and nature so popular? There is something genuinely special about working the soil, creating and nurturing life, raising a living thing dependent on the care you give it, being in partnership with nature, and harvesting and eating fresh, sun-ripened vegetables you have grown yourself. Plants respond positively if you provide proper growing conditions. And plants don't care if you are young or old, fat or thin, white or black or purple with yellow spots.

Thelma E. Honey is a wheelchair user most of the time and a longtime avid gardener from New Mexico. She offers, "Aerobics and gym workouts tone our muscles, including the heart. Walking, running, jogging, and cycling add fresh air and oxygen as well as sky and sun. Gardening gives us all these, plus the tranquility of watching the bees and butterflies and birds. We can also eat the fruits of our labor."

Another major benefit of working with plants is that you always have potential new friends. Garden clubs and plant shows are great places to meet and interact with people with similar interests. My grandparents have made many good friends through their gardening club activities. Nothing gets people talking across the backyard fence quicker than the garden. An interesting experience I had illustrates this point beautifully. After I started working as a horticultural therapist, I established an enabling garden at Chicago's Lincoln Park Zoo, which was then visited by thousands of people every day. The garden was located in an area formerly used for pigs (boy, did things grow!) and in full view of many passersby. The garden was tended by patients from my alma mater, the Rehabilitation Institute of Chicago. I imagine we made quite a sight with all our wheelchairs, electric scooters, walkers, crutches, every manner of race and disability, and gardening stuff all over the place. The real beauty of the garden went beyond the plants because, rather than being avoided or receiving quick sideways glances as people walked briskly by, we were bombarded with attention. People would stop and ask, "Hey, those are nice tomatoes—what kind are they?" or "I wish my soil was that good!" or "What's the name of that plant?" The garden connected us. We were as accepted as anyone else. The common bond of gardening seems to transcend *all* social barriers.

Medical scientists and other researchers have gathered important evidence that exposure to natural environments like woodlands and parks is very valuable to our well-being. Most of us prefer tree-lined streets to those without, but why? Why do people want and use parks in their neighborhoods? Why are our wilderness areas and open spaces so valuable to us? We human beings seem to have an instinctive need to be around plants and nature. Some scientists hypothesize, based on such preferences, that our ancestors evolved in a savanna landscape, where clumps of trees were interspersed with open grassy areas. Trees or woodlands meant safety—a place flee to keep an eye on the grassy surroundings without being seen. The more dangerous open areas were places to hunt but also offered greater risk of being seen as prey yourself. These preferences for open areas dotted with clumps of trees are reflected in the most popular designs in our city parks.

As our abilities to move about change due to age and disability, so do our opportunities to hike the wilderness pathways and to experience the natural areas we apparently instinctively need. They may become less accessible to us. We need to look more at our own yards and gardens for our nature needs. By being involved in gardening, you in effect bring nature to you.

We all know how important rest and relaxation (good old R & R) is to our morale and overall satisfaction in life. What we do for fun can be stimulating, challenging, and rewarding. The opportunities offered through gardening for quality recreation time are nearly limitless.

Plants provide almost immediate, continuous, and long-term rewards: the germinating seed, each new leaf of the growing plant, the slow but steady maturation of trees we planted as kids. Harvesting tomatoes fresh from the vine and warm from the sun, carrying over seed from that

Kelly Conrad, HTT, who manages a horticultural therapy program in Iowa, shared the following from a friend: "I am a 28-year-old male who received a head injury and spinal cord damage during an automobile accident while under the influence of alcohol. During rehab, horticultural therapy was there for me in an inspirational and supportive way. I was given the oportunity to design and construct a railroad tie terrace, which I participated in from start to finish, choosing building materials to be used, deciding on location of terrace, and being foreman of the project. This project came at a positive time for growth of self-confidence, and my self-esteem, grew enough through this project to give me inspiration to want to live once again. I can hold my head high, knowing that my self-worth is worth having."

special squash your great-grandmother used to grow, are deeply rewarding, connecting us with both the past and the future.

Medical scientists and psychologists have also begun to measure and identify physical and mental benefits from participation in garden activities or simple exposure to environments which include plants. Hospital patients require less pain medication and fewer days in the hospital when viewing trees outside their windows, as opposed to looking out on a brick wall. Visits to public gardens appear to lower blood pressure. Increasing numbers of hospitals, rehabilitation programs, retirement communities, and nursing homes are establishing programs that use horticultural activities as a treatment. As a result, the profession of horticultural therapy, which employs gardening and related activities as a therapeutic tool, was established. Most commonly used with people with disabilities and older adults who are undergoing some form of therapy in institutions, it is also used as a vocational training strategy. Gardeners have been getting therapy all along!

Horticultural therapists are specially trained to use their knowledge in part to select gardening activities and equipment appropriate to the abilities of any person who wants to garden. The American Horticultural Therapy Association, established in 1973, is the sole organization in the United States concerned with the promotion of horticultural therapy and rehabilitation programs. The AHTA is dedicated to the development of efforts which serve and train people who are older, disabled, or disadvantaged. The AHTA supports the professional development, education, and enhanced expertise of horticultural therapy practitioners. Horticultural therapy is gaining national recognition and acceptance because of the efforts of the AHTA. Horticultural therapists are located in every state and are an excellent source of help. The Canadian Horticultural Therapy Association has a similar helpful mission for our northern neighbors.

In inner cities across the nation, community garden programs work with neighborhood residents to reclaim vacant lands and transform them into parks and vegetable gardens they manage themselves. These efforts, besides transforming neighborhood liabilities into assets, bring together people who normally would stay behind closed doors, have gotten them talking to one another and organizing to cope better with other issues, such as drugs, gangs, housing, and education.

As I stated previously, those of us who actively garden have known of these many advantages to mind and body that gardening offers. Since the purpose of this book is to encourage each of you to garden no matter what your age or ability, to never have to stop if you don't want to stop, you need to create your own Enabling Garden at home. To do that the first step is to frankly assess your abilities. This will provide the individualized information about how much you want to, can, or should do. You will select special structures and equipment, design the garden, and choose the plants. Most importantly, you will create a garden you can manage, and one which enables you to reap the benefits of gardening for as long as you wish.

Assessing Your Gardening Abilities

The first chapter established that gardening is beneficial to us on many levels. However, many people are unable to garden in common ways due to disability or aging. A thorough understanding of your abilities and limitations, along with basic considerations of body mechanics, will provide the information needed for lifelong enjoyment of gardening. When you understand your needs, you can then select structures and tools, plan the overall design of your Enabling Garden, and learn the best ways to perform the various activities.

Very frank self-assessments are absolutely essential here. There is no point in creating a garden that is beyond your physical capabilities. Take careful notes as you visualize yourself in the garden and as you learn more about making gardening accessible throughout this book. While reading, you may want to refer back to this chapter for further self-evaluation. Your gardening capabilities will certainly improve as you learn to adapt the garden to your needs.

Time, Mobility, and Reach

Those of us who experience a temporary or permanent disability know that life becomes an exercise in adaptation. We make the best use of our abilities along with the assistive equipment we need. We get to be very good at this, out of necessity and from the challenge of overcoming barriers or simply finding easier ways. This applies to the Enabling Garden, too. We need to combine what we know about our abilities with the adaptations that enable us to do what we want to do in the garden. The information in this section will help answer questions like What activities should I do? What should I avoid? How can I be more protective of my body while gardening?

This chapter will help you relate your abilities *and* limitations to various activities in the garden. You will see how to protect abilities you have by avoiding activities that may aggravate an existing condition or cause a new problem altogether. Proper body positioning when working in the garden is also important to health and affects tool and structure selections. Finally, learning your height, reach, and other important physical dimensions will help you select the most appropriate structures, tools, and garden arrangement for you.

✪

Patricia Schrieber (43): "I suffered a severely fractured right ankle four years ago. Since I used gardening as one of my healing therapies, it was very important that I adapt a new way of using a shovel. I use my stronger left foot as my anchor, as I always did when shoveling. However, I cannot use the typical right foot-thrusting motion I had always used previously. That kind of intense impact would cause tremendous pain, and gardening is supposed to be fun. So I use a short, D-handled shovel. I put both hands on the handle, and place my right foot on the top edge of the shovel head. I press down with my foot without lifting it off the edge, while moving the shovel back and forth slightly with the handle. The shovel moves down further into the soil. I continue the two separate motions of

Basic Considerations

The first and foremost gardening consideration is your time. The total time you have available to garden and the time tasks take you will affect most every decision you make from here on. With my disability, no matter how I try, it takes me an hour to get dressed and out the door in the morning, whereas others can do this in 15 minutes. I also work full time and then some, so I only have limited time to garden in the first place.

Considering your mobility and time, you can begin to establish the amount of gardening space you need and appropriate activities. As a wheelchair user, I find it impractical to mow the lawn, and my wife doesn't have the time, so I pay someone to do it. I am also cutting down on my lawn area through other plantings that I *can* care for or that require lower maintenance. The best advice is to start small, with perhaps no more than 30 minutes needed per day to take care of all the garden maintenance without fatigue. The retired person who has good mobility, has more leisure time, and really enjoys gardening can design his or her garden accordingly.

Your overall mobility is the next most important consideration after time. This will indicate what garden components and tools you require and, to a great degree, the overall layout of your garden. Frank self-assessment will prevent you from creating a garden that enslaves you from either a time or an ability perspective. For example, if you have severe mobility restrictions, you may want to locate frequently used areas, such as the vegetable garden, closer to the house so all your energy isn't used up getting to and from them.

It is a fact of life that if you live long enough, many physical abilities will decrease. I always advise people planning a garden around a certain set of "permanent" conditions, therefore, to remember they might change in the future. For example, I know that at some point I will not be able to push my wheelchair over lawn areas; I can barely and slowly do it *now* with my normal hand and arm strength. I have thus planned to enlarge my deck and add an adjacent paved patio that will cover existing grass areas. I will connect these to other areas with additional firm-surface paths, which are much easier than grass to roll on and wide enough to provide great freedom of movement, eliminating higher maintenance and inaccessible grass in the process.

Ability Determination

By comparing the following mobility considerations to your own abilities, you will be able to make better judgments regarding the basic garden components and equipment. These factors will help establish whether traditional ground-level gardening is practical and, if not, what kinds of paving, structures, and tools will make gardening accessible.

Consider your abilities to do the following:

✪ If you are able to get down to the floor and up again without assistance, many ground-level gardening activities are appropriate. Knee pads, padded hand tools, gloves, and a hat will help protect your valuable abilities as long as possible.

- If you must get in and out of the bathtub using your arms to push on the sides of the tub, you can try ground-level gardening. It would be easier, though, if you perform the task from a standing position and use lighter weight, long-handled tools. Otherwise, use a little stool to sit on and, when working at ground level, to provide a platform for pushing with your arms to stand. Again, use knee pads to protect your joints. Gardening on one knee with frequent switches to the other knee is easier on the back and knees.

- If you cannot bend over and pick up a soup can from the floor, have a back problem, or have balance and coordination limitation, avoid or minimize all stooping or bending activities. Use long-handled, light-weight tools for ground-level and some overhead tasks. You may perhaps use a cane for support to help get around and up and down from the ground, but you are still able to walk fairly long distances. Level surfacing may begin to be important, with no hidden potholes or tripping hazards, particularly if you also have some visual limitation or can easily be thrown off-balance.

- If standing on one foot is too challenging, also indicating compromised balance and coordination, or you cannot walk up steps without difficulty, avoid steps and keep all slopes to a minimum. If you use a walker or crutches, you will have difficulty performing traditional garden tasks because you need your hands for mobility. You will experience increasing difficulty carrying things, so you will need special equipment to carry plants and tools. Frequent seating is required within reach of the activity, or temporary use of a wheelchair may be necessary to free up your hands while in the garden. Paving considerations, traction, and drainage are increasingly important for mobility. Raise the soil level to comfortable heights with various containers. Overhead work is also best avoided, indicating long-handled reaching tools and planting areas located within easy reach. Bending at the waist should be kept to a minimum.

- If you use assistive devices for walking, is it possible for you to use the device with one hand while holding and using a tool with the other? If so, careful one-handed tool selection or adaptation is necessary. This is perhaps best combined with raised soil or containers to make gardening more readily accessible. Consider your ability to walk on uneven surfaces and up curbs and inclines for proper path and other surface selections. Hoses and watering cans will be cumbersome to move.

- If you have difficulty walking unassisted on an incline, you may need railings and should pay greater attention to potential tripping hazards. Minimize slopes and choose firm, level surfacing as opposed to grass.

- If you are unable to walk very long distances without fatigue, either with or without assistive devices, then keep frequently visited garden areas close to the house or concentrated within comfortable walking distance. Provide plenty of seats for frequent rests, and position them

pressing down with my right foot and moving the shovel from side to side with my hands on the handle. All the while, my left foot gives the rest of me the support and anchoring I need. I keep on in this manner until I get the shovel to the depth I want. The rest of the digging operation goes as I had done previously, using my upper-body strength to remove the loosened soil from the hole. I recently amazed myself by digging a hole that was close to 2 feet deep and 2 feet wide. I have gained wonderful stamina through this activity. When you consider that my ankle was, in the surgeon's words, 'smashed like a teacup', and put together with a lot of orthopedic skill and five pins, I consider myself to be very fortunate that I have been able to adapt to a new way of gardening."

near areas requiring frequent attention, offering privacy, or featuring engaging views. Again, consider your surfacings within garden areas carefully.

✿ How long you can comfortably stand on your own, with or without assistive devices, is important. The shorter the time, the more seating you need. As seating becomes more necessary, containers and other ways to raise the soil become important, too. Most garden areas will need to be near rest stops or close to the house. Again, a wheelchair may be needed temporarily in order to free up your hands. Raised soil levels help you avoid bending at the waist. Lightweight, portable seating, such as folding lawn chairs, may be appropriate.

Gardening While Seated

At the point where stooping or bending is uncomfortable or should be avoided for medical reasons, hands are increasingly used for mobility with canes and walkers. Working while seated is then increasingly more practical and comfortable than most traditional, ground-level methods of gardening. You can make gardening in these cases accessible through containers, raised beds, and other ways of bringing the soil level and plants closer to you. These methods must be combined with firm, level ground surfaces that provide consistent traction and drainage.

If you are more comfortable while seated, the following considerations regard appropriate tools and methods to bring your garden to you.

✿ If you can get up unassisted from a chair without your hands and stand for short periods, you will want to position seating at frequent intervals around the garden, employ more containers, and use trellises and other vertical gardening techniques that take advantage of the extra reach you gain by short periods of standing. If possible, you might carry lightweight seating with you in the form of a small stool or folding lawn chair. Reaching aids will help extend your limited reach when seated.

✿ If you must use your arms or chairs with armrests to stand, it is important that the soil is at accessible heights. Use heavy or stable containers and other structures in the event that you must use the structure *itself* for support (see Chapter Four). This is also important where general balance or coordination is compromised. Consider proper tools that comfortably extend reach. You may need to create raised beds with built-in seating space.

✿ If you can bend over while seated and pick up a can of soup, you can use this ability for some minor hand weeding or to simply pick up a dropped object. If that is not possible, use various reaching aids that pick up dropped things and extend reach without requiring bending. Again, comfortably position your soil and plant.

Compensating for Limitations

Such seemingly insignificant abilities as reaching the ground while seated can dramatically reduce the reliance on containers and other structures that raise the soil. A planter box only 1 foot high may be quite easy to tend for the seated gardener with the ability to safely bend at the waist.

❂ For those who use wheelchairs to get around all or the majority of the time, traditional, ground-level gardening is difficult, particularly if the trunk, arms, and hands are impaired as well as the legs. The paraplegic (loss of use of the legs) with "normal everything else" can be amazingly active and participate in a wider range of activities than many people think; in the garden many activities require little or no special equipment other than tools that extend reach. As mobility and function decrease, however, you may need increasingly sophisticated devices in the garden, as you might around the house for eating, grooming, and dressing. The person who uses a wheelchair also requires firm, level surfacings, with appropriate inclines and no steps. You will need to raise most planting areas and use adaptive tools to improve your capabilities. Larger paved areas also give greater overall freedom of movement. Leave plenty of uncluttered open space for easy turning and overall mobility. Find lap trays and other devices to carry things around in the garden. Hoses are difficult to handle, so they must be conveniently positioned and appropriately equipped.

❂ If your hands or arms are weakened through injury or arthritis, you may require gloves or padded, "fatter" tool handles (see tool section). Heavier loads are best avoided. Hoses will be more difficult to move around, so position and equip access to water carefully, or consider installing automatic systems. You will need various gripping aids and wrist supports, along with generally smaller, lightweight tools.

❂ Various levels of visual impairment affect all aspects of gardening to some degree. Use bright, dramatic color, form and textural contrasts for tool handles and plant combinations. Equally important will be safe surfacing with no tripping hazards and easily found entrances and other features to avoid confusion. Suggestions for visually impaired or blind gardeners are found in several sections of this book.

Measuring Workspace Needs

No matter the similarities in our abilities and gardening positions, our height and reach limits are varied. Those illustrated here are for *average* humans and from both standing and seated positions. With a partner and a tape measure, measure these limits for your unique size and shape. Also consider different positions.

The average measurements for a wheelchair user are also included, but models vary in size, particularly those used by children. Electrically powered chairs and scooters, used by both children and adults, may require larger paved areas for greater freedom of movement. The turning radius will be important to know for the wheels of the chair and the overhang of the feet. Check reach limits with your arms out to the side, straight out in front, and overhead. The arc of your reach overhead to side and front is also important for positioning overhead objects and designing plant support systems, such as archways or other trellis structures, that follow this dimension.

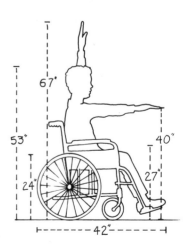

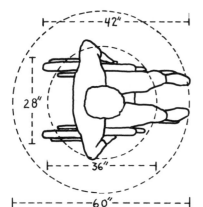

Along with time and degree of mobility, consider your overall strength and endurance—both for now and what it may be in the future. Strength and endurance affect mobility and the time it takes to perform tasks. While the garden is a great source of exercise and physical challenge, our strength and endurance will limit us, no matter who we are. As you consider this fact, concentrate your energies on fun, important garden activities and let someone else mow the lawn.

*B*ody Mechanics and Efficiency

No matter what your limitations and abilities, and no matter what gardening activities you choose, there are steps you should take to limit your risks of strain and injury. Weakened or older joints are easily strained, but you can minimize everyday risk with proper body positioning and a basic understanding of body mechanics.

Work Factors

Repetition Repetitive tasks performed over long periods can overwork muscles and tendons. Arthritis is particularly sensitive to prolonged, repetitive tasks. Weeding, harvesting, digging, and dead-heading spent blossoms can all be repetitive over long periods. By performing these tasks for shorter lengths of time, and mixing them with less strenuous tasks or simply changing hands and positions frequently, you can protect yourself to a certain degree. Proper tools and equipment are also important. For example, use pruning shears that are both comfortable and sharp.

Force   Force is the exertion required to do a job. If very great force is required, something might give. Improperly positioned or equipped, it's usually us. You can reduce this risk factor by proper posture. For example, we've all been told to lift something with the legs, not the back, and to hold the weight close to the body. On the other hand, with added leverage, sharper, smaller bladed tools, well-amended, easily worked soils, and many other adaptations, you can use your strength wisely by minimizing the force required to do many garden tasks. You can also distribute force over stronger, or more, body parts by using two-handed tools rather than one hand alone, or using legs instead of your back.

Posture   The way you position your body while working is critically important to safety in the garden, as anywhere else. Awkward positions invite injury. Select tools and equipment that permit proper and neutral body positioning, such as with your wrists straight rather than bent. Use both hands to distribute force and provide greater control. Permit your hands to remain close to your body while working, rather than with arms outstretched. If bending or stooping should be avoided or is impossible, use long-handled tools or consider container or raised-bed gardening as better alternatives.

Increasing Efficiency

Proper body mechanics are critically important to your working abilities. Repetition and force can be lessened and posture corrected with consideration of the following body mechanics.

✪ Choose the proper tool to reduce the force required of you.

✪ Keep your arms low and elbows close to the body to maximize strength and avoid strain.

✪ Keep the work as close to your body as possible. The farther away from your body you hold or work with something, the harder it is on your shoulders and back.

✪ Lift and carry heavy loads, such as watering cans or potted plants, at waist height with two hands, if possible, and avoid repeated bending and lifting.

✪ Bend your legs and keep your spine straight when picking up things from the ground, along with holding the weight close to your body. Avoid bending at the waist with your knees straight, especially if you are lifting something off the ground, as opposed to bending to sample the fragrance of a flower. Bending at the waist is probably one of the riskiest movements for those with back or leg weakness. Avoid bend-

ing and lifting repeatedly or for extended periods of time. Keep hoses on reels and small pots on shelves. Grow vining crops that climb up to meet you rather than you climbing down to the ground to tend them. You can customize the height of containers and raised beds to virtually eliminate back strain while tending plants.

❁ When seated, keep your spine straight, not slumped forward, and use seating with lower back support. Increasingly available in sporting goods stores are excellent lower back support belts that can be worn while in the garden. Check with your doctor if you have any questions. Better to be safe.

❁ Avoid holding any single posture too long—mix it up! Activities that require grasping, bending, standing, or sitting should be frequently changed to avoid repetition, strain, and overwork. Otherwise, muscles will quickly become overloaded; with decreased blood flow, pressure on joints and sensitive skin increases and becomes painful.

❁ Reaching overhead with both arms and looking upward can cause back strain or loss of balance. Reaching overhead with one arm is safer.

❁ When standing, try to "get a leg up on the competition" by using a foot rest. Placing one foot on a 6- to 12-inch stool or horizontal surface decreases strain on your spine and legs. Even strategically placing a few rocks of various sizes in the garden provides this benefit in an unobtrusive and attractive way.

❁ Use a technique called "sit-lean-stand" when getting up and down from any chair or garden bench. Seating should have arms for pushing up when standing, if needed. Optimal chair height is also a consideration: The distance from the ground to the seat of your chair should be around 19 inches, depending on your height.

Other individualized risk factors may include your tolerance to heat and cold and your overall physical condition in the first place. You may also be taking medications which affect capabilities. This is why it is important to consult your doctor and therapist before engaging in any new activity they have not previously specifically approved. It would be wise to consult a physical, occupational or horticultural therapist at some point in this initial assessment process. They understand disability joint motions and body mechanics and will be able to help you select proper body positions, tools, and structures that adapt you to your planned activities while minimizing risks.

It is strongly advisable to do some stretching or warmup exercises before working in the garden. I hesitate to recommend specific exercises because your routine should be approved by your doctor or therapist for your individual needs.

The information here about capabilities, limitations, and body mechanics should now prepare you to make wise Enabling Garden structure, tool, and plant choices.

Getting Around:
Paths and Surfaces

3

This chapter covers how to adapt your garden to suit your needs. This means keeping the garden *functional*. Practicality, access, and budget will dictate what materials you ultimately use. The goal here is to continue gardening.

With the information you determined about yourself in the previous chapter, you are ready to select the various structural components that make your garden accessible to you or any other gardener. These components will form the "hardscape" or bones of your garden. For many, Enabling Garden structures, including paved areas and plant containers, will be the dominant features that make the garden accessible in the first place. Therefore, careful selection of the various elements and their construction materials is important so the finished products are both functional and looking like they belong together.

If you have good mobility, the information in this chapter will probably exceed your basic needs but will still offer ideas you can adapt to your situation. The ideas here, along with the tools suggested in Chapter Five, will enable you to keep gardening comfortably for many years to come.

*P*aths and Surfaces

If you use an assistive device for walking or use a wheelchair, you're going to have to carefully consider all paths and other surface areas in the garden. Let's face it: If you can't easily and safely get to and from your garden and move about in it, you probably won't enjoy the experience very much.

The most common surfacing material in the garden is grass. For many older gardeners, grass is an effective surfacing material. For people who use wheelchairs, however, a good, healthy lawn is very difficult to roll through, due to its padded, giving nature—much the same as a thick shag carpet. Too, crutch and cane tips are easily caught in grass, so it is generally avoided in the Enabling Garden except as an accent or in areas you do not need to visit regularly. Grass may also conceal uneven ground that could throw you off balance. Of course, the resiliancy of grass does cushion accidental falls, more dangerous on hard surfaces. In many cases, though, a hard-surface paving is absolutely needed. Consider the following important factors when you select paving for your garden.

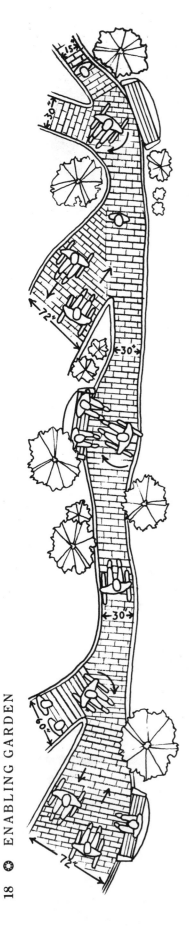

Paving Requirements

The paths and paved areas must be smooth, level, and firm. Canes and tires must not sink in. There can be no uneven edges on which a person could trip. Wood chips are a common path material but are inappropriate for people who use wheelchairs because they are too soft and giving. It is important that loose materials, such as stone or gravel, be firmly packed.

Provide good traction at all times. Never use materials on which water can pool, a situation that could promote slippery algae growth or ice, an obvious winter hazard. Wood is particularly slippery when wet. In general, good drainage or quick drying is a must. Textured surfaces, rather than "smooth as glass" surfaces, promote good traction.

Paths, ramps, and other grades should not exceed 5 percent. This means that every 1 foot of change in slope height requires 20 feet of path. Even less slope is preferable on long paths as long as proper drainage is maintained. Larger flat areas, such as decks and patios, are properly constructed with just enough slope to carry away water. Most manuals give 8-percent slope as a maximum, but 8 percent is very demanding for a person who uses a wheelchair and is best applied only for curb cuts or other short ramps. Obviously, these grade recommendations could be exceeded for those with greater mobility. Also, steps in the Enabling Garden should generally be avoided.

Handrails may be necessary as a barrier on sloped paths and other areas or if additional support is needed for safety by the gardener with compromised balance.

Proper width of paths will be dictated by your needs and to a certain extent budget. I generally recommend using the minimum navigable width for paths which simply connect one garden area with another. For me, 36 inches is the bare minimum path width that allows me to turn my wheelchair around; this keeps my wheels on the path, while my footrests hang over the edge. I have a friend, however, who is 6 foot 6 inches tall and uses an electric wheelchair. He requires a minimum of 5 feet to turn around if foot clearance is okay. For two people to walk side by side, 5 feet is recommended, and 6 to 7 feet allows two wheelchairs to pass. Budget will be a factor because it is relatively expensive to pave an area, so minimizing lengths and widths reduces costs without compromising mobility.

One suggestion that accommodates various needs and is more interesting from a design perspective is to widen and narrow the path in different locations. This will provide path locations that allow adequate turning radius for wheelchairs or placing seating.

Provide direct routes through the garden. If you may become disoriented or have visual impairments, paths should have a clear beginning and end, with fewer private areas with the house out of view. A windchime or another audible feature may be useful for orientation.

Paths should have a sharp textural contrast at the edge, such as concrete to grass, so people with visual impairments can detect the edges. Raised edging, such as of wood or brick, may be necessary if there is a danger of wheelchairs or strollers rolling off the path. Also, some types of paving must be contained by an edging material to prevent shifting.

Raised edging could create tripping hazards, though, and should be even or flush with the paving.

Provide a large paved area, such as a patio or deck, as a place to cluster plant containers and other structures. This also gives you a lot of freedom of movement among your plants.

Use a textural change across the path as a signal to people with visual impairments. This can indicate an entrance to the patio, a tree with interesting bark, or a clump of particularly fragrant plants. The indicator strip must be flush with the existing surface so as to not create a tripping hazard. The strip should be about 12 to 18 inches wide and made from any noticeable contrasting paving material, such as a brick strip across a crushed stone path, as long as the change in texture to serves the purpose.

Reduce glare and heat absorption. These qualities are greatly influenced by color. Glare is uncomfortable for most anyone and is at an extreme in full sun on bright surfaces, such as concrete. Use such surfaces in shady areas only, if possible. Dark surfaces, such as asphalt, absorb heat, however, and may make the garden uncomfortable at certain times of the day. They do melt snow and ice and dry quicker after rains, which is an advantage in some areas.

Resiliency, or ability to cushion falls, may be important for garden areas frequented by children, ones with potentially dangerous features, or when the gardener's balance is compromised. Concrete, at one extreme, lacks resiliency, in comparison to grass lawns, wood chips, and other organic materials. Some newly available synthetic surfaces are firm enough to dribble a basketball on, yet cushion falls and permit access to wheelchair users without wheels sinking. You can see these most often in newer children's playlots at schools and parks.

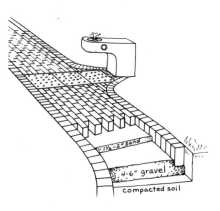

Soft Surface Options

Once you have determined the dimensions and other criteria of the paths and larger surface areas in your garden plan, you can evaluate the many options for paving materials. Each has its own aesthetic merits, ease of installation, practicality, and cost. Cost is often influenced by local availability; if the material is manufactured locally, chances are it's cheaper. Consider less expensive options in remote or less visible areas, such as the path to the compost area or the vegetable garden, as opposed to an attractive patio adjacent to the house. The material should also be low- or no-maintenance once installed.

The following list is by no means exhaustive, but you can apply the criteria discussed above to most any surface. The bottom line is that it must provide safe and easy access to, from, and around the garden.

Turf   Grass is a viable surface option as long as it provides safe access in the garden. It certainly is inexpensive. Although grass's resiliency offers more cushion than brick if you happen to fall, this very characteristic makes mobility almost impossible for the person who uses a manual wheelchair. On the other hand, electric wheelchair and cart users can bulldoze their way through just about anything, and turf doesn't seem to be a great obstacle other than during the wetter times of the year. I have found that when there is no snow cover (which is actually a great deal of the time during Chicago's winters) but the ground is frozen, the lawn is quite easy to get around on using my wheelchair. This is hard on the dormant grass itself, though, so should be minimized.

Grass is cooler than hard surfaces and does not create a glare problem. It does require plenty of maintenance, including regular core aeration of walked- or rolled-upon areas. In addition to creating a thicker, healthier lawn, aeration tends to even out the inevitable lumps and bumps caused by freezing and thawing, which could create a tripping hazard.

Rather new on the market, is a unique process whereby a grid of inert material, such as recycled plastic or even rubber from old tires, is placed over specially prepared soil. The open spaces within this grid are seeded with grass. The surface is more durable than a regular lawn and provides the firm surface needed by people who use wheelchairs. I'm looking forward to personally evaluating this because turf paths are attractive.

Wood Chips   Unfortunately too readily available and commonly used as nature trail paving in parks and woodlands, wood chips are produced when logs and branches are run though a chipper. I say "unfortunately" because in my neighborhood wood chips become available through the death of a tree. Sometimes, tragically, a perfectly good living tree is "executed" because it was planted too close to a house or under utility wires, where it later became a hazard. We need all the trees we can get! But that's another story.

Chips are generally available free (in areas with lots of trees, anyway), are attractive, and will usually eliminate weeds if applied about 4 inches thick. They are fine and comfortable for walking in any area used solely by people without mobility impairments.

In the Enabling Garden, however, wood chips are best relegated for use as mulch around plants, for which they are excellent. They are too soft for easy crutch, cane, or wheelchair access. Furthermore, because wood chips are organic, they readily decompose, requiring constant renewal.

Packed Soil   Certainly a surfacing option. This depends greatly on what the soil is composed of and the general climate. Soils heavy in clay or organic matter have obvious disadvantages when wet. You can use such soils more readily in arid areas than in areas with ample rainfall. Pure sand, the opposite type of soil, is usually unacceptable for surfacing other than beaches and children's playlots. Though it cushions falls, it does not provide the firm surface needed in the Enabling Garden. Essentially, packed soil is only an option where it naturally drains well and remains sufficiently dry so it isn't tracked around too much of the time. The soil should be compacted to prevent erosion and weed growth.

Crushed Stone and Gravel

Packed crushed stone or gravel offers perhaps the best low-cost surfacing alternative for the Enabling Garden. When a good selection is properly installed, this material provides excellent drainage, year-round traction, low maintenance, and long life. The key is selecting the best materials from the many available. Installation, while important, is essentially the same for each material.

Installing crushed stone or gravel requires excavating to a depth dictated by your local soil and drainage conditions; usually at least 6 inches is necessary. The material in the bottom of the excavation must be compacted to prevent later settling. Various landscape fabrics can be used to line the bottom and the sides to minimize mixing of the soil with the stone and to inhibit weed growth. The stone material is applied, leveled, and thoroughly compacted. The finish grade should be slightly below the surrounding grade, both to contain loose material and to allow easy mowing along the edges. At added cost, various edging materials can also be used to contain the stone, but they must not create a tripping hazard. High-quality plastic, steel, or aluminum edging could be used where grass or groundcover plants tend to creep into the paving.

Your loose aggregate material (the fancy term for gravel) *must* be *crushed* stone, which is angular. Crushed stones are mixed *sharp* pieces, of which the largest pieces are about ½ inch in diameter, with all the fines left in the mix. This is opposed to roofing (river or pea) gravel, which is composed of uniform, pea-sized, rounded stone, with no fines at all. The stuff cannot be packed down. I've seen it used for paths in parks, and you should hear the mothers with toddlers in strollers as they quickly become imbedded in this stuff.

Using material with the fines mixed in allows it to be packed down to form an almost solid surface. The fines fill in the gaps between the larger pieces, and the larger pieces tend to present a flat face to the surface, creating an almost solid pavement. These larger pieces also weigh enough to fall by the force of gravity alone when wet without sticking to shoes, crutch tips, and tires. Mixes that contain too many fines tend to be picked up on everything when wet and are easily tracked around because each individual particle is too light to drop—a major disadvantage.

By its very nature, gravel never totally binds together. Loose pockets can form within firmer areas, especially after freeze-thaw cycles, allowing tires and so on to sink, or creating a slipping or tripping hazard.

Such disadvantages can be minimized with careful selection of materials and proper installation, including *thorough* compaction.

Inspect the inventory of your local construction material suppliers to help determine the best materials for your area. The following are some of the choices you will be offered, but remember: "Crushed to approximately ½ inch, with the fines mixed in."

Crushed Limestone   This crushed material has an almost snow-white color that I find disagreeable. It is generally composed of pieces from approximately ¼ inch in diameter down to dust. In the Chicago area limestone is very cheap because it is one of the predominant bedrocks. When properly installed and dry, the stuff really binds together except for the very top layer. When wet, though, the limestone tracks around everywhere. The dust in the mix tracks white footprints and tire marks, and shoes and wheels look almost as though they were painted. Limestone is used between cold frames where I work, and it sticks to my wheelchair tires like you wouldn't believe. Materials like this, with too high a propor-

Soft Surface Paving Options

	Advantages	Disadvantages	Comments
Turf, grass	Cheap, attractive, cooling effect, okay if ambulatory	Maintenance required, too soft for wheelchairs, and strollers, destroyed in high-traffic areas	Not recommended as "enabling" paving
Wood chips	Cheap, attractive, readily available, okay if ambulatory	Readily decay in wet climates, require replacement, too soft for wheelchairs or strollers	Apply minimum of 4 inches deep
Compacted soil	Firm surface when dry, cheap if native materials used, low maintenance if compacted	Tracking when wet, soft when wet, erosion	Must drain well, better in dry climates, must be compacted for firmness
Crushed limestone	Readily available, cheap, firm surface when compacted, low maintenance, good traction, drains well	Mix too fine, poor color, bad tracking problem when wet	Not recommended
Decomposed granite	Firm, level surface when compacted, appropriate mixture of coarse and fines, attractive color, low maintenance, good traction, drains well, inexpensive relative to hard surface paving	Always *some* loose material on surface, which could be slippery; good surface for wheelchairs and strollers; could be more expensive than other crushed stone	Highly recommended
Screenings or number-nine crushed stone	Firm, level surface, good mixture of coarse and fines, inexpensive, drains well	Always some loose material, could be slippery, good for wheels, color a bit bright	Recommended

tion of small pieces in the mix, should be avoided. A mix of crushed limestone with pieces that are too large is more difficult to pack down during installation. This is liable to create a washboard effect that is murder to roll over and does not meet the criteria of a firm, *level* surface. It also has a high pH so when used where soils are already alkaline it enhances the problem.

Decomposed Granite   Probably my material of choice for making less expensive paths or other paving if budget is a primary concern after function. I have seen this weathered granite rock a great deal in mountainous areas on major park trails or as surfacing on other high-traffic areas. In our area it is red-brown, which is much more attractive than other options. It has a neutral to slightly acidic reaction in the soil, which is another advantage here, where alkaline soils are a challenge.

Number 9 or Screenings   Around Chicago there are many gravel pits where retreating ice-age glaciers left their moraines, or deposits of loose gravel, behind. These deposits are excavated, crushed, separated, washed, and graded for sale. Almost a by-product of the process are screenings, or number 9 stone, which makes excellent paths. It usually comes from a mixture of parent rock types, so it may have a mixture of colors. In my area it is definitely off-white, because limestone is dominant in the mix. The primary disadvantage of screenings is its highly reflective color, which in sunlight is bothersome to sensitive eyes. In my view, garden paths should be used but not seen to the point of distraction.

In the final analysis, compacted crushed stone can be attractive and inexpensive paving material. It does a pretty good job of meeting our surface criteria. I feel it is useful for remote areas of the garden, connecting paths, and areas where appearance is not so important, such as in the vegetable garden. Its main limitation is its invariably loose surface. This problem can be avoided with the following hard surface options.

Hard Surface Paving

The natural choice for customizing Enabling Garden surfacing is hard surface paving. The many options available include not only the obvious concrete or asphalt, but also brick and paving stones, which are equally functional but more attractive (with varying costs). As you keep in mind the practical considerations of your barrier-free garden, you may find that hard surfaces are the way to go for the areas immediately adjacent to your house. Loose materials there would tend to be tracked indoors. Properly installed hard pavement should be safe and not require maintenance.

Hard surface paving offers these advantages:

- ✪ Better control over drainage and final grade during construction
- ✪ Excellent traction (most surfaces)
- ✪ Either smoothness, as long as good traction is maintained, or texture, for better traction and more interest
- ✪ Attractive color selections that reduce glare and heat absorption
- ✪ Comfortable walking or rolling at any time of the year
- ✪ No tracking of loose material into the house or garden

The primary disadvantages to hard surface paving are its relatively complex installation and higher material costs. A contractor will likely be necessary, a situation which introduces an additional labor cost.

Color is an important consideration when selecting hard surface paving. Plain concrete reflects a great deal of sunlight, which may be uncomfortable for some older adults and people who are visually impaired. At the other extreme is asphalt, which absorbs a great deal of heat, making a garden uninhabitable for both plants *and* humans in certain climates, at least during certain times on a hot, sunny day.

On the whole, hard surface paving, when affordable, is the pavement of choice in most Enabling Gardens. The following sections evaluate various materials. As with loose paving materials, using what is manufactured locally is a possibility to lessen cost.

Concrete   Probably the first thing you think of when you think about hard paving surfaces. It is definitely hard, level, and comfortable to walk or roll on. During construction, you can control drainage, grade, and surface options to improve safety and appearance. This is particularly important for larger areas and those adjacent to your house. Given the choices available, plain, white concrete should be avoided if possible, because it reflects a great deal of light. It's also ugly compared to many other options that cost approximately the same. Unless installed fairly thick and reinforced, concrete tends to crack when used in larger areas such as patios, creating a tripping hazard. Regularly spaced expansion joints can minimize this but can create tripping hazards all their own.

Of course, if you already have a large concrete patio, I would not suggest that you replace it. Concrete may be fine in shady areas, and when *professionally* installed should be problem free.

Recognizing how boring plain concrete is, manufacturers have created many new surfacing options that make concrete more versatile and attractive. You may want to consider:

✪ **Brushed** This is simply a roughening of the freshly poured surface, usually with a stiff brush. This most simple option improves traction, reduces reflected light to a small degree, and should always be used because it is safer.

✪ **Exposed Aggregate** A pebbled surface can be created after the cement begins to harden by gently rinsing and brushing away the top layer to expose the aggregate in the concrete. You can order concrete mixed with different colors of aggregate to give you a custom look. I have also seen this surface effect created by embedding various colored pebbles, even in patterns, in wet cement.

✪ **Mixing Materials** You can set brick or stone accent strips into fresh concrete to create interesting patterns or simply break up large areas. I do not recommend wood because it will decay before the concrete needs to be replaced, leaving dangerous gaps that are difficult to repair.

✪ **Decorative** Dyes can add color, and pattern molds add texture, when pressed into wet cement. You can create a look closely matching brick, paving slabs, cobblestones, and other interesting patterns. Such techniques are a bit more expensive than pouring plain concrete, but worth investigating if you choose concrete.

Asphalt Asphalt is the most common general paving material after concrete. Where readily available, it is cheaper than concrete and makes a firm, comfortable walking or rolling surface. It is effective on roads, driveways, walkways, and bike paths.

Again, if you already have asphalt don't take it out, as long as it is in good shape and safe. However, when you have the choice, it is better to spend your money on the many alternatives available, even though new asphalt costs less than concrete.

As a paving surface in the Enabling Garden, asphalt has several disadvantages:

✪ **Absorbs Heat** By nature of its dark color, asphalt paving becomes very hot in full sunlight. Unless there is a consistent breeze, any large surface may become uncomfortably or even dangerously hot. Plants in containers placed near asphalt tend to dry out much quicker.

Phoenix is not the place for an asphalt patio. In colder areas, however, snow, ice, and rain melt and dry quicker on asphalt than on materials with lighter colors.

✪ **Poor Long-Term Durability** The various tar components in asphalt tend to "evaporate" or degrade in full sunlight over time. With less of this binding material holding it together, asphalt starts to break up. In higher traffic areas such as roads, vehicle wheels tend to repack the surface, helping the material last longer, but the surface still ultimately cracks. Once this happens, water gets underneath. In colder areas, this is the deathknell for an asphalt surface: Repeated freezing and thawing rapidly breaks up the surface. This is why sealing is recommended at least every two years to maintain the necessary moisture barrier and lengthen the life of an asphalt surface.

✪ **Tends to "Move"** Asphalt is somewhat flexible—it bends rather than breaks, particularly when heated by the summer sun. Applied at the thickness generally used for driveways and patios, asphalt suffers from freeze-thaw action that, combined with summer softening, fairly quickly causes pockets where water collects. In extreme cases, an uneven surface with lumps and bumps forms, which could be a tripping hazard. Asphalt is also easily damaged by tree roots because of these flexible qualities.

Some, if not all, of these problems can be avoided if the asphalt surface is installed over proper base preparation, and the asphalt itself is applied thickly enough. With that, however, the cost per square foot goes up, making asphalt comparable to more attractive and equally effective options.

Loose Pavers   Pavers are generally installed loose (without mortar between joints) by being placed into a layer of sand. Loose pavers are the most versatile and desirable paving option in the Enabling Garden. Versatile, because they are available in just about any shape, texture, and color, allowing you to create interesting patterns by mixing and matching various types and sizes. Loose pavers are also made of a wide range of materials, including bricks and slabs made from baked and fired clays, concrete, natural quarried stone, and asphalt. These surfaces are desirable because they drain well, have excellent traction, and offer comfort and safety to people who use wheelchairs, canes, and walkers. They can also make transitions in grade gradually because the smaller units can be installed without abrupt height changes.

Loose pavers offer the opportunity to add great warmth and character to your garden. If you use a wheelchair, you may cover a significant amount of the garden surface with paving to provide greater assess and mobility. In this situation the dominating surface can be made attractive and in character with your home or the type of garden you are making.

The proper installation of pavers is both critical and hard, work perhaps best left to a professional contractor. A properly excavated and compacted soil base is covered with a layer of compacted, coarse crushed stone, followed by a layer of leveled sand specially used for this purpose. Edging of some type is critical to contain the paving materials and prevent

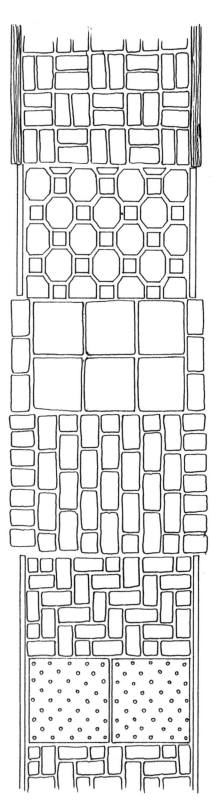

them from shifting over time. Finally, the pavers are installed in the desired patterns, with sand again worked into and compacted between gaps in the pavers until they are filled. You can take pavers to the next step in durability (and expense) by setting them in and filling joints with mortar. This will also eliminate weeds in the gaps between pavers. Pavers for patios and walkways should be 2⅜ inches thick, while driveways or patios with heavy plant containers should use those 3⅛ inches thick.

Brick Available in an incredible variety of colors, brick is perhaps the most versatile paver. By nature of their small size, you can lay bricks in many patterns to reveal your creativity and add interest and character to your project. Along with traditional clay, bricks are now made from concrete and even asphalt. Some manufacturers offer interlocking pavers, which are shaped to mesh together, minimizing gaps and shifting. These make excellent paving materials. Laid end to end, bricks can create a visual sense of direction. A contrasting color edge or a texture strip serves as an indicator for people who are visually impaired.

Other Pavers Pavers come as large as several feet across, very useful in covering larger areas. They are available in many natural and man-made materials. Natural stone or any quarried material is more expensive than pavers made from concrete or asphalt. Like brick, other pavers are available in a nearly infinite variety of colors, textures, and shapes that permit your imagination to run wild. Perhaps even more interesting is to mix larger pavers with smaller ones—creating a personal design that also indicates important locations, such as entrances or features of interest for the visually impaired gardener or visitor.

Extra care is necessary when installing larger pavers: If unevenly supported from below, they may crack under heavy loads, such as large plant containers. Smaller pavers are more forgiving because there are more joints in the surface.

Wood One of the most popular additions to a home a wooden deck. A deck offers the large, firm, level surface that may be necessary for greater mobility in the Enabling Garden. Wood adds, for me, a natural feel, warmth, and character to a garden. In areas of the country where trees are harvested, wood is an economical choice as well. It also stays cooler in the sun than other hard surfaces. Wood's main disadvantage is that exposure to the elements causes it to deteriorate. When in contact with the ground or exposed to *full* sunlight, even rot-resistant wood will ultimately decay. Specially milled lumber must be used for decking to minimize the warping and splitting that creates tripping and sliver hazards. Exposed wood must be sealed, painted, or protected some other way from the elements, which adds maintenance cost and a greater time factor. Wood is also quite slippery when wet and promotes algae growth in damp shady areas that will stay wet longer because of wood's porous nature.

Ultimately, the surfacing material and style you select must provide the essential, basic access to and around your garden. With comfortable mobility you have eliminated at least half of the physical barriers to gardening itself.

But simple access is not enough. Most places advertised as accessible to people with disabilities, are simply that—there are proper grades, wide and firm paths, designated parking, and wonderful surfaces with minimal steps. The rose I want to smell, however, is too far away. The fruit is too high to pick or the ground too low to plant seeds comfortably from my wheelchair.

The next chapter will really give you the "meat" of creating an Enabling Garden—one which goes beyond mere access to allow you to participate in the many wonders of gardening.

4

Adapting the Garden:
Raised Beds, Containers, Structures, and Vertical Gardening

Sandra Foreman, HTM, suggests replacing up to a third of the soil in large containers with polystyrene peanuts used as packing material. This saves up to a third of the weight, making containers more portable and safer on rooftops or balconies.

*E*nabling Garden Structures

Now that you can easily get to and around your garden, the single most critical gardening adaptation for many people with disabilities and older adults is to raise the soil level to a comfortable working height. Raised beds, and other plant containers filled with easily worked soil mixes, offer the key to successful gardening for as long as you wish. This may mean little more than mounding your ground-level planting beds, say 10 to 12 inches high, so that they are within easier reach. Or planters and raised beds on or adjacent to paved areas may be necessary. For many of us the latter, in combination with well-considered tools, offers the best option.

Once you can easily reach the soil, the need for other adaptive equipment is really minimal. However, the flip side is that with carefully selected tools (discussed in the following chapter), you may not need as many structures. In other words, structures can lessen the need for special tools, and special tools can lessen the need for structures. The optimum for most people is a little adaptation of both.

Again, the ideas offered here may not be appropriate for everyone but should be adaptable to your needs. The do-it-yourselfer with reasonable access and ability to use tools should be able to make many of the following ideas.

Treated Woods

Wood in contact with soil and moisture has much longer life with protectant compounds, applied under pressure to penetrate the wood, that seal out moisture and inhibit the growth of decay-causing microorganisms. The current literature shows that these chemicals *do* leach into the soil for potential uptake by plants and—if they're vegetables—by you, too. These chemicals are toxic and, as they are leached from the wood, many feel that they present hazards to the environment in general and should not be used in the garden at all.

There are varying grades of pressure-treated lumber. It is recommended that you ask your dealer for the proper type for the job. Wood treated with creosote, toxic to plants and humans, should not be used. An exception is *old*, recycled railroad timbers, which are sufficiently aged to avoid problems.

To be safer, don't select new pressure-treated wood with chemical residues on the surface, which may be washed into the soil. Wear gloves when handling new wood during construction, and a dust mask and safety glasses when cutting it. Avoid growing vegetables and other edible plants in containers or raised beds made with pressure-treated wood for a year or two, until any residual surface material is weathered away. Various wood sealers can be applied to minimize exposure, and some suggest lining the container with plastic as an additional precaution. Deck manufacturers often recommend you avoid walking barefoot on new decks for some time. Yearly partial or complete soil changes can further minimize this hazard, but to my knowledge there are no recorded cases of harmful effects from eating vegetables grown in containers made from treated wood.

Some general suggestions when building plant containers and other structures with wood:

- Use screws instead of nails whenever possible because the swelling and shrinking of wood exposed to weather gradually loosens nails.
- Be sure to protect exposed wood from rapid moisture gain and loss, the major cause of warping and splitting, with paint, stain, or sealers. I prefer those that permit wood to weather to a natural color while providing protection.
- Be sure all rough edges are rounded or sanded to avoid slivers. All wood that may come in contact with people, in my view, should be periodically checked for sliver hazards.
- Always use rot-resistant or pressure-treated wood to avoid quick decay of surfaces in contact with the soil.

Raised Beds

Raised beds are generally permanent garden structures that contain a large amount of soil. Because of their size, they are usually not portable, unlike many other plant containers. They are essentially bottomless boxes, built to contain soil but open for drainage below. In the Enabling Garden they provide ready access. Because of their relatively high cost, though, you should concentrate them in active areas requiring frequent attention. The vegetable garden would be the first place to build raised beds, which would make little sense in a low-maintenance shrub border, for example.

Always build raised beds as large as possible, but allowing the gardener to reach all areas. Adding 12 inches of width to a free-standing raised bed 3 feet wide and 10 feet long increases the square footage by 33 percent. There is only a minimal increase in cost because of the additional 12 inches at each end and the extra soil to fill the greater volume.

A raised bed offers the following advantages:

- You can customize soil height. This helps minimize bending at the waist, and provides access to gardening for people who can't easily get up and down from the ground or if ground-level gardening is beyond reach, as is the case for many wheelchair users.
- Contains a larger area of soil, so a wider diversity of plants can be grown in them. The largest bed will support small trees.

- Requires less frequent waterings by virtue of its larger soil volume and, therefore, greater moisture-holding capacity.
- Generally quite durable, lasting many years with no maintenance.
- Stable and heavy enough for you to sit on the edge or lean on for support without moving or tipping.
- Offers the most comfortable access to a greater amount of gardening space for the person who uses a wheelchair or must sit while working.
- Warms up quicker in the spring than ground-level beds, enabling you to get a quicker start in the spring garden. Here in Chicago, onions, peas, radishes, lettuce, and more can all be planted a month earlier.
- You control the soil mix, which can be ideal for your intended plantings (see Chapter Six).
- You can raise short plants up to eye level. Public demonstration Enabling Gardens are very popular because *all* visitors can see, touch, or smell plants close up.

The disadvantages of a raised bed:

- Cost and complexity of construction.
- Its permanence means you must carefully consider location. Also, you must build it to withstand year-round outdoor stresses over the long term.
- Being bulky, it tends to dominate a landscape, particularly ones 20 inches or higher (but remember, practicality over aesthetics!).
- Generally requires a seated gardener to work to the side, which may be difficult. A table or roll-under planter might be more appropriate (discussed later).

Size Bearing in mind average height and reach limits (Chapter Two), a raised bed for a seated gardener or one using a wheelchair should be about 2 feet high. But a range of 18 to 30 inches might be okay.

- 18 inches—Comfortable if you wish to sit on the edge of the bed itself while tending plants. In this case, a wider platform is necessary along the top. This is also a good height for a child's range of reach.
- 24 inches—If you are seated in a chair or bench next to the bed, including a wheelchair, this is about the best height. It minimizes back strain and maximizes reach into the bed itself. The standing gardener may lean against the side of the bed as well for support. And most bending at the waist is eliminated, depending on how tall the person is in the first place.
- 30 inches—This is the best height for the standing gardener who cannot bend at all, but is too high for most seated gardeners and young children.

The width of the raised bed is also very important. If the bed is accessible from only one side, it should be a maximum of 30 inches wide. Seated, you should be able to reach the rear of the bed easily. Standing, you may be able to have a wider bed because you can lean over it to a certain extent. This general width is appropriate for a raised bed built against a fence, along a wall, or wherever the ground on the other side slopes away too dramatically to be accessible.

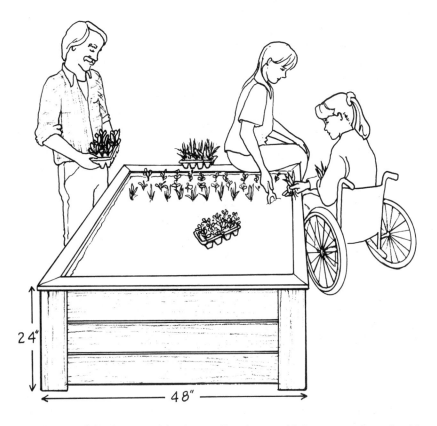

24"

48"

A raised bed accessible from all sides could be approximately 60 inches wide. The average standing or seated gardener working from either side of the bed should be able to comfortably reach the center.

If you want to sit on the edge of the bed while working, or just to use it for general seating in your overall design, it must be wide enough to be comfortable. Eight inches is about the minimum, but 16 to 18 inches is standard for general seating. However, walls this thick take away from the wheelchair user's reach. Therefore, where bed wall seating is not necessary, choose construction techniques and materials that make the wall as thin as possible (without compromising long-term durability). This is important because the thinner the walls, the more square feet available for gardening by either the seated or standing gardener.

To maximize the raised bed's square footage of soil, I would also consider designing it to take advantage of my extended reach *with* the tools I typically use. I am thus able to add 8 inches of bed width beyond my fingertips, because I am seldom without a trowel or hand cultivator while working at a raised bed.

When deciding on the measurements for a raised bed, sit parallel to a table, your legs not underneath it, and measure how far you can reach into the center. This gives the approximate width of a one-sided raised bed. Double this for a bed accessible from both sides. If you prefer standing, lean comfortably into the table, with your thighs against it and measure. The key here is comfort. Use one hand to support yourself on the table, as you would in the garden. Be sure you think about how long you may be able to actually work in the position you choose.

It may look weird at the table, but go through the motions of gardening with your tool and take measurements. This is going to give you very important information, resulting in raised-bed and other garden dimensions customized to your specific abilities.

The simplest raised bed, and one I have used around my own garden, is made by simply berming or mounding the soil so that it is 10 to 12 inches higher than the surrounding surface. The width was dictated by how far I could reach with my tools, a good 5 feet. This small elevation of the soil makes gardening much more accessible for anyone, especially when combined with proper plant and tool selection. The inevitable areas not easily reached, even with special tools or structures, should be planted with very low-maintenance plants.

I have tried this berming technique in a small vegetable garden, but I still find the soil in this labor-intensive area too low to manage effectively. For many of my retired friends, though, this simple adaptation makes all the difference in the world. I have found this height to be fine in beds where I keep shrubs and perennials requiring less frequent attention. Also, a raised bed this low doesn't require walls or edging to hold back the soil because it gradually tapers down to ground level. If you require more than 8 to 10 inches, you will need some sort of material to contain the bed. The higher you go, the more complex the construction.

You can even design an aquatic garden in a raised bed, bringing an added dimension to your garden. Other raised beds, however, must provide the good drainage that most plants require.

You can construct raised beds from a wide variety of materials, ranging from concrete to wood to masonry and just about anything else you can get that is reasonably durable (that won't rot out for a couple of years, anyway) and will hold soil for healthy plant growth. Landscape timbers are probably the most commonly used material for building raised beds. Construction techniques vary in different parts of the country, and as the construction complexity increases, so does the cost. On average, raised beds cost approximately $4 to $6 per square foot to build, including soil.

At the Chicago Botanic Garden's Enabling Garden for People with Disabilities, raised beds were constructed in 1976 from various materials. The purposes were both exhibiting the materials suitable for raised beds and evaluating their long-term durability. All of the beds were constructed 24 inches high and ranged in width from 20 to 60 inches. The weather extremes of Chicago made for an excellent test laboratory. The materials included these:

- ✪ Stacked flagstone
- ✪ Vertically placed landscape timbers
- ✪ Hortizontally placed landscape timbers
- ✪ Pressure-treated 2 x 10-inch lumber
- ✪ Cedar wood in several styles
- ✪ Concrete or cinder blocks
- ✪ Reinforced concrete paving slabs

Stacked Flagstone A cheap material here in Chicago. It is generally quarried from limestone deposited locally in loose horizontal layers, easily split apart. Flagstone is often used for stepping stones and even set in sand or mortared together to surface a patio. The basically irregular pieces range in thickness from 1 to 3 inches. The faces are lumpy and bumpy, which helps them lock together when stacked. However, it is generally too rough for paths and surfacing in the Enabling Garden.

In our raised bed, roughly rectangular pieces were selected so that the finished wall would be about 12 inches wide. (The rear of the bed was walled with landscape timbers backed up to a fence). The flagstone walls were stacked so the joints overlapped for strength, even without mortar. To keep the bed from gradually falling out into the garden due to freeze-thaw action, each layer was staggered less than an inch toward the interior of the bed; when finished, the wall sloped toward the center.

This wall's slope, combined with the width, makes it prohibitively difficult to work the bed while seated alongside. The stones themselves are also quite rough, which may be irritating to sensitive skin.

However, the flagstone-walled bed is excellent for the reasonably active, mobile person. The planting area is easily reached with long-handled tools, the wall offers a sitting platform (at least for short periods), and the wall also doubles as a step for comfortable leaning into the bed.

In the Chicago Botanic Garden trials, the flagstone bed has proven to be very durable. It has been planted with thoroughly mulched dwarf shrubs and conifers, which require minimal maintenance. It is a good alternative for the active person, or as a low-maintenance bed for someone with limited mobility and reach. One other problem I have observed, which may be a local phenomenon: Yellowjackets take up residence there, nesting between gaps in the stones. Not easily discouraged once they move in, they can make for one nasty experience in the garden!

All varieties of loose, or mortarless, walls using stackable stones are approximately equally effective for raised beds in the Enabling Garden. They give a natural look to the finished product and can be made almost any shape because of the small, stackable pieces. Pockets left between stones can be planted to soften the overall appearance.

Landscape Timbers Generally made from hardwood, cut 6 x 8 inches x 8 feet. Other sizes are available, and there are such shape options as rounded logs. You can use recycled railroad ties, but they must be old enough that, when warmed in the sun, they don't smell of creosote, which is toxic. I would much rather smell my flowers than that stuff, anyway.

Untreated wood of most any kind, except perhaps clearheart redwood and other expensive tropical woods, quickly rot when in contact with moist soil. Even rot-resistant cedar won't last long. The old saying, "a dead tree will stand forever, but once it hits the ground, it's gone in a hurry," is very true. One of the best rot-resistant woods, and today rare and expensive even if you live in the lower Mississippi Valley and Gulf Coast, is cypress, the tree that can literally grow in water. In the past, greenhouses and their benches were often made with cypress because of its unmatchable resistance to water damage. If you can salvage some from an old greenhouse being demolished, you are lucky indeed. In lieu of this, you should use wood which has been pressure treated to resist decay.

Because they are widely available, relatively inexpensive, easier to work with than other materials, low-maintenance, and durable, landscape timbers are often the material of choice for building retaining walls in a landscape setting and are a good choice for raised beds in the Enabling

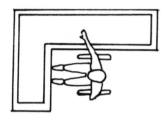

Garden. Raised beds are bulky and coarse in the landscape, and, unfortunately, so are landscape timbers. However, I prefer wood, as opposed to concrete or stone, which can cause damage when my wheelchair rubs against them.

The most common cut is 6 x 8 inches on a side. If seating along the top is important, stack them with the 8-inch side up.

Landscape timbers placed horizontally can build angular beds in many different shapes. You should avoid too many 90° inside corners, however, as these are the least accessible to people who use wheelchairs. Another technique worth trying, although more difficult, is to place the timbers vertically rather than horizontally. This enables you to create truly curved raised beds and avoid inside corners.

In any case, after the timbers are cut to size, they are best predrilled, then nailed together in place with 3/8 x 12-inch spikes. If you need a structure like this to garden, you probably can't put this in the do-it-yourself class of projects. Most landscape contractors, though, are very familiar with this type of construction.

At the Chicago Botanic Garden in 1976, both horizontal and vertical techniques were used, and both styles are very solid today. The only deterioration observed was some significant slivering on the exposed upper surfaces, which ultimately required fastening a 1 x 10-inch plank over the top of the timbers to maintain safety. All wooden containers and structures which come in contact with people should be checked regularly for this problem. Sand or plane to remove the hazard.

In summary, for all-purpose, very functional raised beds in the Enabling Garden, landscape timbers offer a good, durable option.

Cinder Blocks and Concrete Blocks Again readily available and a relatively inexpensive building material. Many masonry contractors are familiar with appropriate construction techniques. Special attention must be paid to preparing a proper footing and maintaining each course absolutely level.

The blocks are usually hollow, which reduces weight, although special solid ones can serve as the top course of the wall. This creates a sitting platform and also keeps debris out of the hollow blocks. Some gardeners might leave the hollow blocks exposed, which would create planting pockets to fill with soil.

To me, cinder blocks are ugly. They reflect a great deal of light, and if exposed to moisture and freeze-thaw action, ultimately fall apart. Cracking from freezing is the primary disadvantage to any smaller masonry wall in contact with the soil or moisture. Frozen moisture begins to crack the mortar joints, which must be repaired or the wall will quickly crumble. This is what happened with the Chicago Botanic Garden example. You can seal out moisture to lengthen the life of the raised bed, but this adds cost and is an unnecessary chore if, in the first place, you select other materials that avoid the problem altogether.

Brick and Other Masonry Very attractive. You can build with bricks or stone made for exterior walls and are therefore very durable. However, a relatively expensive option. You can create just about any shape of bed: The small units can gradually make curves. Masonry walls generally should be built by a professional contractor, but they are not out of the realm of a good do-it-yourselfer. As with cinder blocks, fairly strict construction techniques are necessary. You must take special steps to seal out moisture in colder climates. Not only does it shed water better than a chemical sealer, a stone coping at the top of the wall also provides a smoother seating platform. As anywhere, you get what you pay for, and a first-class construction job should last a lifetime. Brick and other stone walls offer an effective raised bed option, if your budget allows.

Reinforced Concrete Paving Slabs One technique used very successfully in the extreme temperature ranges of both Chicago and Denver botanic gardens is reinforced concrete paving stones or slabs. They are stronger than plain concrete because of steel wires or rods running through the interior. This extra strength enables larger units to be manufactured. The ones in Chicago are 36 x 24 inches and range from about 1 to 3 inches thick. They were placed side by side and sunk 12 inches into the ground, leaving the 24-inch wall needed for wheelchair access. The pavers were secured to a pressure-treated 4 x 4 running along the top inside edge by drilling two holes in each paver and securing with ½-inch bolts. Vertical 4 x 4s—cut 5 feet long, sunk 3 feet into the ground, and bolted to the horizontal 4 x 4 provided additional support. All hardware was countersunk for safety and invisible from the exterior of the bed.

While uncomfortable to sit on, these walls are thin, offering access to the largest area of soil possible.

Wood The Chicago Botanic Garden demonstration used red cedar for several raised beds and other structures. It also makes a very attractive container, whose durability depends upon the thickness of the cedar. In a raised bed where the largest cedar boards were 2 x 4 inches, the walls lasted for 14 years without need of repair.

Although red cedar is becoming increasingly expensive, it offers an

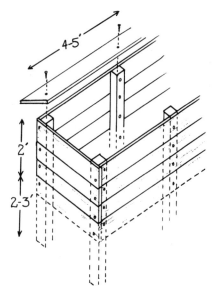

attractive alternative. Its natural, weathered gray color blends well with many home and garden styles, as well as with plants.

Redwood is certainly a rot-resistant alternative, but I have elected not to use this wood because it is essentially a nonrenewable resource. Redwood should be used for more important things, if at all.

Pressure-treated wood is perhaps the most economical material for building a raised bed, durable enough to be considered permanent, and perhaps my material of choice. It is much less expensive than cedar or redwood, and by virtue of its chemical treatment has actually proven to be more durable in the trials I have monitored. Because of its greenish color when new, it is less attractive initially, but this weathers to a neutral grey on exposed surfaces.

Our example in Chicago was walled with 2 x 10 planks stabilized with 4 x 4 posts and capped with a 2 x 6 plank. All assembly was done by predrilling holes and using bolts with lock washers and nuts. All hardware was also countersunk for safety.

Other than cost and durability, another advantage of pressure-treated wood is that the thin-walled construction enables the raised bed gardener to get up close to the soil. The long-term durability of pressure-treated wood means less bulky material can be used in construction. A a 2-inch thick pressure-treated plank will last as long as an 8-inch landscape timber under the same conditions. Our bed has performed very well, with no signs of deterioration since it was built in 1976. The only change I would suggest would be for any raised bed over 10 feet long (ours is 20 by 5) to have a turnbuckle in the middle to pull the long walls toward the center. This will prevent the soil, as it freezes and expands, from evenutally bowing out sides.

You can use wood, pressure-treated or not, to build a wide variety of raised bed styles. The bottom line is that they should offer comfortable access to the soil. A very effective raised bed that makes gardening easier for many people can be made from 1 x 10-inch or 2 x 12-inch lumber to build simple square or rectangular boxes over the existing soil. It is surprising what a difference even 12 inches of additional height makes.

Other Materials   I have visited enabling gardens throughout the country and gathered information on European and Australian ones. They have used materials as the following.

Plywood Where the reach limits of the gardener call for the thinnest walls possible for a raised bed, marine exterior-grade plywood at least $\frac{1}{2}$ inch thick works, provided support is added to counteract the natural flexibility of the plywood sheet. Plywood was used on a rooftop garden at a Philadelphia rehabilitation hospital, where weight was a concern, and stone, landscape timbers, and other materials were impractical. Plywood enabled larger areas to be developed in the gardening program than could be permitted with fewer and smaller containers made from heavier materials.

Recycled Plastic Timbers Landscape timbers made from recycled plastic should become more readily available. This would certainly be a material to consider because of its obvious environmental benefits, but also because it works. They can be cut or drilled for assembly like wood. They are heavier and more expensive than wood and generally of a darker color, which tends to absorb heat. Their long-term durability is unknown.

Interlocking Stone Blocks In the last few years, in an effort to get away from typical landscape timbers and the high cost of masonry retaining walls, manufacturers have developed a system of uniformly molded concrete blocks that are locked together by rods through holes. They thus stack snugly without mortar. The blocks can have a quarried natural stone look or other surface texture molded into them. They are relatively thick but are effective in a raised bed for a standing gardener with greater reach or where the bed doubles as a retaining wall.

Formed Concrete In the Glass Garden at the Rusk Institute in New York, an ingenious method was used to make raised beds 18 inches high. Concrete was poured into molds that gave designers total control over bed shapes and sizes. Wall thickness varied from 4 to 16 inches, accommodating both people who wanted to sit on the edge and those using wheelchairs who wanted to get up close to tend the plants. A terra cotta dye was added to soften the concrete's coloring. The beds were shaped with gracefully meandering curves and as kidney-shaped islands that are very attractive. An expensive option, but formed concrete is worth mentioning.

Aquatic Gardens You can make one in a raised bed to grow pots of waterlilies or other aquatic plants. Simply support a rigid pool liner by an outside framework, or line a rigid wood frame with a rubber liner made for aquatic gardens.

Most raised beds beyond 12 inches high are considered permanent structures. You may not need them forever, because your broken leg will heal in time, but if you are going to raise your own vegetables this year, ground-level is out. You can even make a temporary raised bed by enclosing soil within bales of straw. Once you no longer need the bed, you can compost the straw or incorporate it into your garden as mulch. The point is, anything goes if you must keep gardening. Even though raised beds offer access to the greatest amount of garden space, they are large, can be difficult to build, and simply may not be within your budget. You may not want that much growing area, or they are just too heavy for your townhouse balcony. The best solution in these situations may be to use smaller containers, which still bring the soil up to a comfortable working height, but simply on a smaller scale.

Containers

A container is anything that holds soil and is large enough to support the healthy growth of a plant. Containers are valuable wherever ground-level beds don't exist, such as in inner cities or on apartment balconies. Because you have control over the soil in them, containers can eliminate such garden problems as poor drainage or soil-borne diseases.

In the Enabling Garden, containers are an important way to raise soil to a comfortable working height, offering the access to gardening that may not exist any other way. Containers are basically smaller versions of raised beds, although some containers are very heavy and large enough to support small trees. They are available for purchase and construction in any height needed for accessibility. They are generally thin-walled, lighter, and more portable so they can be rearranged, to highlight particular plants during their best seasons, for example. You can place smaller containers within reach on even simple structures like planks placed on cinder blocks. Such shelves offer greater access if you have a temporary mobility impairment, such as a broken arm, and are easily disassembled when the need has passed. Containers specially made for plants come in an infinite variety of colors, textures, sizes, and styles. Additionally, many items made for other purposes can be recycled as plant containers. You can easily make still others yourself.

You can incorporate containers of many kinds into the Enabling Garden. Due to the wide variety of options available, you should consider the following criteria when evaluating them.

1. Accessibility　This is obviously our first and foremost consideration. Without easy access, there's little point to using the container. For example, a 6-inch pot on the surface of a patio is very difficult to tend from a wheelchair. Placed on a platform of appropriate height, though, it is easily accessible. As we said with raised beds, 24 inches is a good average height. However, once you determine your comfort range, you can place containers at varying heights within that range, giving interesting spatial movement to your garden.

The vertical elements discussed later come into play here, too. You can hang containers on walls, arbors, fences, and railings to add both interest to the design and valuable square footage of growing space. This is particularly important in smaller areas, where every inch must be used efficiently. Hanging baskets with ropes and pulleys allows you to lower them for tending, then to raise them back out of harm's way.

As with raised beds, container dimensions should not exceed your easy reach from any side.

2. Stability　For those of us who use canes or walkers or may easily lose our balance, containers should be heavy enough or firmly attached so they don't easily move if leaned upon for balance or support. They should also withstand a reasonable wind without tipping. This adds an additional margin of safety.

3. Size　Containers come in any size, from thimble-size to huge ones that support trees and shrubs. Bear in mind that the smaller the container, the quicker it dries, particularly when the plant matures and its roots fill the container. Small containers may require watering twice a day on hot, windy days. Worse still, as some plants grow, they tend to act like umbrellas and actually shed water away from themselves when it rains!

A few smaller pots, mostly in the shade, are all I have in my garden because I'm not home enough to tend them regularly. Keep most smaller containers in the shade and use more large containers, which have larger moisture-holding capability. These tactics will buffer a missed watering or allow you to go on a weekend trip without disasters.

4. Durability   Use containers that will last. You want to garden, not be running around repairing and replacing deteriorating containers, especially large ones. Use rot-resistant wood. Bushel baskets will last about one growing season when filled with soil and could be used for temporary needs. Avoid surfaces requiring painting. The container material must withstand constant contact with moist soil and repeated freezing and thawing. Many fired clay pots, even larger ones, cannot withstand freezing and must be emptied each winter or they will crack. If in doubt, ask the manufacturer or avoid the product, rather than risk winter damage.

5. Weight   is an important consideration for plant containers, particularly in a rooftop or balcony situation. If you expect to move the containers around your patio to feature different ones or tend them, they must be light enough for you to do this either independently or with help. When assessing weight, don't forget to add the additional weight of the moist soil and plants.

Smaller, lighter containers avoid the weight problem but generally need to be placed on or hung from various structures for easy reach.

6. Appearance   With the infinite variety of materials and styles available, you should be able to select containers that blend well with your home and garden. I would select colors that don't detract from the plants in them. In other words, containers should be seen but not heard. However, as I said earlier, anything goes if it provides accessibility in the Enabling Garden—old pedestal bathtubs make whimsical, accessible planters. Recycled tires can be stacked to provide a great place to grow vegetables. The possibilities here are literally as limitless as human creativity.

I prefer the color of weathered wood. Color is an important consideration with containers in full sun, since dark colors absorb heat and will become hot to the touch. White is very reflective and should be avoided, especially if it compounds the glare from a concrete surface. Natural earth tones seem to work best outdoors.

7. Cost   With the wide variety of manufactured, recycled, and do-it-yourself container options, comes an equally wide spread in cost. Because plant containers may be the backbone of your Enabling Garden, try not to cut corners here. To maximize the amount of garden space available to you, consider buying three lesser quality but larger containers, as opposed to one of ultra-high quality that shorts you in volume or square footage. Conversely, ten very small containers will not be as useful in the long run, requiring more frequent waterings, as fewer, larger ones.

Manufactured Containers

Manufacturers have long recognized that plants are very popular both indoors and out. Plants indoors usually require containers; for millions of apartment dwellers, containers are the only option. Visit any garden center worth their salt, and you will find a plethora of plant containers made from wood, metal, clay, ceramic, plastic, and stone, in almost every imaginable finish.

Redwood and cedar are the most common woods used in the familiar octagon-shaped tubs and other boxes. They are made up to 24 inches in diameter and 18 to 24 inches high and therefore meet our accessibility criteria. Smaller window boxes are useful on railings, shelves, and attached to fences with brackets.

Plastic containers are generally lighter in weight and lower in cost than comparably sized containers made from other materials. Some of late look just like clay pots. Bear in mind that some plastics become brittle when exposed to winter weather and can easily crack. Some plastics also deteriorate when exposed to sunlight: Ultraviolet rays can damage the molecules in the plastic, causing fading or brittleness, so these containers are best used in shady areas of your garden. Plastic containers manufactured with ultraviolet inhibitors are the best. Still, no matter how disguised, plastic is still plastic, and while it is fine where weight and cost are limiting factors, I prefer more natural materials.

The standard **clay** pot is also common, and its terra-cotta color is very attractive. They are made in large sizes that can be placed directly on the garden surface and still be at an accessible height. In cold winter areas, empty them before they freeze, because they tend to crack.

Clay is porous, allowing air and moisture exchange through the pot's sides, so it will tend to dry out quicker, even in a shady garden. Even though there's nothing nicer than fresh, new clay pots, this porous quality ultimately causes unsightly staining or even algae growth on the sides, although some manufacturers treat the containers with sealers and inhibitors to control this.

Clay is also molded into many more decorative styles, with some made to hang on fences or walls. There are strawberry barrels, various bowls and shallower pans, and even animals. Because of the neutral terra-cotta colors, the more unusual shapes are not too detracting from the plants.

One container I particularly like because of its rustic look is the **oak whiskey barrel**. In areas near distilleries, these effective containers are readily available. They are recycled to garden centers after the bottling process and usually cut in half. I have found them to range from 18 to 22 inches in height, making them a good option for the Enabling Garden—and at around 12 dollars each, a pretty good bargain. In Chicago they last at least 5 years before rotting out. I have used them at home to grow many a fine crop of tomatoes; two full-sized plants can be grown in each one with a teepee trellis.

Depending on how fresh the barrel is, you may still smell alcohol, which is toxic to plant roots. If so, you should fill it with water and let it soak for at least 24 hours. This soaking is aided by their usually not having drainage holes prior to sale. Unless you want a water garden (which is certainly possible), you should drill five equally spaced, 3/4-inch holes in the bottom.

Another container option using a full-sized barrel starts with drainage holes as above. Then cut 2½-inch holes roughly 12 inches apart all around the barrel, from top to bottom. Fill the barrel with soil, then set small transplants into the holes. Many vegetables and annual flowers and herbs can be grown in them. I tried growing strawberries this way, but they were killed during winter. Perhaps greater success can be achieved in warmer areas of the country, than Chicago.

Flue tiles and drainage pipes Among products manufactured for other purposes yet adaptable for Enabling Garden plant containers are flue tiles and drainage pipes. Made of clay with some coarse sand mixed in, and fired longer and hotter, they are somewhat harder than regular clay pots. Their side walls are also thicker, which lends additional strength.

Flue tiles are normally stacked end to end to line chimneys. They are generally square or rectangular, 24 inches long, and range from 10 inches across for homes to 24 inches for large factories. Terra-cotta colored, they closely match standard clay pots and blend well with plants.

Drainage pipes are made from the same material, and also in 24-inch lengths. The pipes are round, however, ranging from 8 to 36 inches in diameter. They have a flange at one end that enables one to overlap the next when laid end to end in a trench.

When flue tiles and drain pipes are placed on end and filled with soil, they make excellent, accessible plant containers in the Enabling Garden. They are a good height, heavy enough in larger sizes not to tip over, very durable, good-looking, and relatively inexpensive. Both are available from larger construction material dealers. They range from $8 to $60, relatively inexpensive for their size. Since neither type is designed to be plant containers, they are not guaranteed for use as such. I mention this because even though I have used hundreds of them over the years, and for the most part they have proven very durable, once in a while a batch of them is not fired long enough or had wetter than normal clay going into the kiln. Such a tile or pipe will not hold up to winter freezing and thawing. This is rare, however, and worth the gamble because they are so inexpensive. Even a bad one will last a few years before breaking apart, while some of mine have been in use for over 15 years.

I generally prefer the larger sizes because they provide the most growing space and, being thicker walled, are more durable. They will not tip over when filled with soil, as opposed to the smaller sizes. The largest ones, 24 inches in diameter, weigh about 200 pounds empty and 400 pounds filled with soil. They will not blow away, but they sure could ruin your day on a weak rooftop or balcony! These are better used on the ground. Another disadvantage of the smaller ones is that when the soil freezes, it not only expands toward the top but also pushes against the bottom. This action lifts up the smaller containers, letting soil escape from underneath. This requires annual emptying, setting them flush to the paving, and refilling.

Flue tiles and drain pipes must be placed on level surfaces for a seal to form around the base to trap the soil. Enough of a gap still remains for excess water to drain away unhindered. You can place such a container off the edge of the paving if you place it on a paving slab with matching dimensions to prevent settling. You can also place tiles and pipes adjacent to one another to form larger beds, create barriers at edges of pavement, frame benches, or develop interesting patterns.

The large round pipes look best and are more effective free standing and accessible from all sides. These aren't the fanciest containers, but they do the job very effectively at modest cost. I feel that you should consider them, when available.

Exposed aggregate concrete Recently available in sizes appropriate for the Enabling Garden, these containers, made from concrete poured into molds, have an exposed pebble finish. They are quite heavy. The exposed aggregate is very rough, which may be irritating to sensitive skin, but it does soften what would otherwise be a stark concrete appearance. Several color options are available in the pebble finish. The most appropriate size I have used, which costs about $100, is 24 x 24 x 24 inches. I have seen some 24 x 24 by up to 72 inches long—virtually a ready-made raised bed—but these are extremely heavy, requiring cranes to move into position.

Homemade Containers

If you are reasonably capable with tools or have a friend willing to help, you can make many of your own plant containers and other useful structures to make your garden much more accessible. Making containers yourself enables you to customize their sizes and shapes to suit both particular design situations in your garden and your unique requirements for accessibility. The following examples are wood, but if you have an interest in pottery or ceramics, try classes to apply your creativity to making smaller plant containers. Again, use anything that is accessible, holds soil, and drains well.

You can get additional homemade container ideas in the many books, videos, and magazines on garden design, garden structures, and container gardening specifically. Always bearing in mind your needs for accessibility, you can adapt many of these ideas for your garden. The resource section in this book offers some excellent sources I have used over the years. The best sources even include the construction plans. I have also found that once you begin creating your own Enabling Garden, you will become sensitive to how you might adapt ideas from plant containers you see on city streets and sidewalks, in malls, and around buildings where soil is hard to come by. You'll also look more closely at other gardens where designers have used containers to add both dimension and essential greenery. Use your surroundings as a source of valuable ideas.

Not being a carpenter myself, I defer to those who are and to the hundreds of available woodworking books, always following the guidelines for rot-resistant wood. The ideas that follow are *basic*, perhaps to the point of primitive, but if you've got table saws, routers, and the skill to use them, go ahead and make virtually anything you wish—all the better. The point here is that many useful containers can be built to bring the soil within reach.

All of the container dimensions illustrated should be regarded only as general *guidelines*. A few inches difference to customize a container to your needs may make all the difference for access. You can certainly change dimensions to conform to your unique garden design situation, too, as long as accessibility is maintained.

Boxes The easiest containers to build are simple variations on squares or rectangles. You can tailor the height, length, and width of boxes to suit any space or accessibility requirement in your Enabling Garden. Smaller boxes are suitable to hang on walls and railings or placed on shelves at the heights you require. Larger ones, placed directly on paved surfaces, offer not only more growing space but easier portability than raised beds, permitting everchanging workspace and display designs.

You can make a larger box even more portable by attaching *heavy-duty* casters to its bottom, or placing the box on a strong platform with casters. Casters that lock are essential for safety. If you use casters, be sure to figure them into the planned height of the container. Use rot-resistant or pressure-treated woods, weatherproof glues, and rust-resistant screws and bolts rather than nails where possible. All containers should have drainage holes, unless noted otherwise.

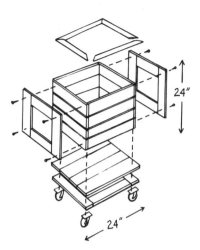

Box with Chains on Fences and Walls   One simple idea that enables the seated gardener to get his legs under the container is to suspend it from chains hung on a fence or wall. They are generally a maximum of 24 inches wide and as long as you wish—bearing in mind the strength of the supporting fence or wall. There must be approximately 27 inches of clearance underneath. The box itself is only 6 to 8 inches deep. I have used this method very successfully in a partial shade situation. I fear that in full sun, however, the shallow box would dry out quickly, so grow plants you won't lose if they dry out once in a while.

Trough Garden   This container is very easy to make from three 8-foot lengths of 2 x 12-inch lumber. It is 24 inches high and 6 feet long, with a 12-inch open space underneath for toe clearance. A gradual narrowing in width from top to bottom makes the container less boxy looking.

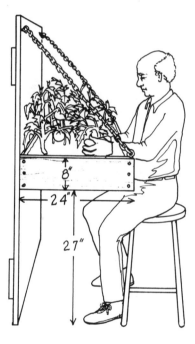

Window Box Fence   This structure supports window boxes and can be made in several variations. It can serve as a barrier or fence, though it will not provide total privacy screening. It can also frame a garden entrance or section off one area of the garden from another. You can adjust the window box height to the perfect level for you. With hanging baskets included to soften the overall look, this project can make a very attractive addition to your Enabling Garden.

Trellis Box   Another versatile container is this rectangular box made from 1 x 12-inch lumber, 15 inches wide, 12 inches deep, and any length you want; ones 4 feet long are still light enough to move fairly easily. The trellis is made from 1 x 2 slats with a 2 x 4 frame. It is then attached with a single bolt at the center of each end of the box. This bolt, when loosened, allows the trellis to pivot and be adjusted to lean against a wall or stand vertically. Two units built with a 4 x 5-foot trellis can be positioned about 30 inches apart, with the trellises leaning against each other and tied together to form an A-frame that allows a person using a wheelchair to roll underneath. This feature makes it easier to reach and tie vines, such as tomatoes, onto the trellis and later harvest them. This structure will also support a spectacular array of flowering vines.

Note of caution: When this or any other freestanding trellis planter is covered with plants, it can act almost as a sail in a strong wind and more

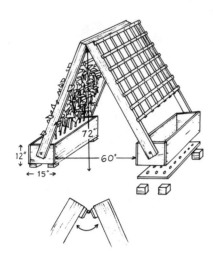

easily tip over. You can add support legs for greater stability, but they may create a tripping hazard. Otherwise, where you expect strong winds, you could anchor the structure off the edge of the pavement, drive spikes through the bottom of the box and between gaps in paving slabs, or use anchor bolts in solid pavement.

Another option is to attach the trellis framework to a wall or fence, with accessible containers placed or built at the base. The containers in this case must be no more than 12 inches wide so you can get close enough to reach high into the trellis to tend plants. This option reduces portability, but *always* think safety first. Various combinations of containers and trellises offer a great deal to the Enabling Garden. They are versatile, bringing plants within easy reach for tending and harvesting, but most of all they make a dramatic impact when covered with lush greenery and fragrant blooms.

Plants in ground-level beds at the bases of walls or fences can even be made "accessible" through trellises or vine nails in walls. Other plant supports simply bring ground-level plants within easy reach. For example, my wife, Cathy, plants my tomatoes in a ground-level bed for me. I place stakes over the plants to support them, do the tying, and lo and behold, the first cluster of fruit ends up about 15 to 18 inches off the ground, within easy reach. As the plants mature, I tie them higher and higher, and it gets even easier to harvest one of my favorite treats of the summer. This technique can be used with many taller or vining plants, particularly in the vegetable garden.

Seating Very important, I believe, in any garden, but especially in the Enabling Garden, where lack of endurance may require frequent rest stops. Most importantly, seats are for when the work is done and you can sit and "smell the roses," enjoy the visits from butterflies, birds, and other wildlife, and observe the day-to-day miracles with which your garden rewards you.

Many garden construction books show several very attractive designs for combining seating and plant containers. Seating next to containers offers anyone a convenient platform for tending the plants. You can fine-tune the measurements to create valuable components for your Enabling Garden. The person using a wheelchair has ready access to the planters, as do people using the built-in seating. All garden seating must drain well and dry quickly, unless you like cool surprises! Avoid dark colors in full sun, unless you like hot surprises as well.

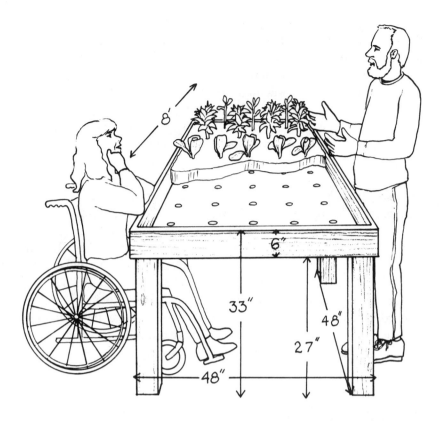

Table Planters This easily made container is especially recommended for wheelchair users and other seated gardeners. A shallow soil-filled tray is supported on legs making approximately 27 inches of knee clearance for gardeners using chairs to scoot underneath. Again, you can customized the height to your requirements. The important thing is adequate clearance underneath. Make the box no wider than you can reach, depending on how many sides are accessible. The soil container should be a minimum of 6 inches deep, making the structure's overall height approximately 33 inches. The top of the planter should be no higher than the seated gardener's rib cage.

Accessibility measurements are a bit more critical with this type of container because it has a couple of drawbacks. If these are accommodated, the many advantages for accessibility make these containers worth a try. The main drawback is that the shallow soil limits you to shallow-rooted plants. The 6-inch soil depth is the minimum needed, but most plants perform better in deeper soil. Plants that are taller and normally rooted deeper tend to topple over in the wind when their roots are too shallow.

Another limiting factor is moisture. The shallow container dries out very quickly in full sun, particularly as the plants mature and their roots fill the soil. This requires automatic or drip irrigation or, at a minimum, very frequent waterings. Therefore, these table planters are more suitable in areas of the country that are cooler, more humid, and with regular rains. In warmer, windier, and less humid locations, keep these containers in shadier areas or planted with plants tolerant of dry conditions.

In a situation where you want to stand and lean against the container, the soil can be up to 12 inches deep if you build a *strong* support system to bear the extra weight. Adjusting the length of the supporting legs would enable you to raise the soil level to about your waist when standing. The increased volume of soil will hold more water longer, permitting a greater diversity of plants. These containers can make a very useful addition to the garden, because you can make them virtually any size as long as they are accessible and adequately supported. In the right place, you can't go wrong with a table planter.

Stairstep Bench   This is one of the easiest ways to display smaller containers very effectively at an accessible height. You basically build a staircase with plastic-coated wire mesh for the steps. The first step is 12 inches high, with the third, top step at 36 inches. Each is 8 inches deep. You can create a beautiful display by placing a collection of smaller pots on the steps. As the plants mature, a solid wall of color is possible. This structure has been very effective in a shady spot at the Chicago Botanic Garden. It also works in the sun if you have the time to water frequently or fill it with cacti and succulent dish gardens in decorative clay pots. This method also brings tiny plants into easy reach.

Vertical Structures

When considering the major structures, the bones, of your Enabling Garden design, you should consider fences, walls, and arbors. Besides their basic functions of defining areas, screening, making boundries, providing support for plants, and offering shade, these vertical structures can provide greater access to gardening space. You can hang planters on and train plants to them, thereby bringing more plants within reach, especially important if you have mobility limitations. Careful selection and incorporation of these structures into your garden will also lend added dimension and beauty to the site.

Walls and fences traditionally screen and divide one section of the garden from another. They can and should be incorporated into the Enabling Garden. In addition to providing support to plants and containers, they can screen unwanted views, be a barrier to strong prevailing winds, and create sheltered microclimates that are more comfortable for you and permit you to try more sensitive plants. For example, at the base of my south-facing garage wall, my snow crocus and snowdrops (*Galanthus* spp.) are always the first blooming in my neighborhood in the spring. These first signs of spring are important to me after being cooped up all winter—they're sure signs of exciting things to come! Look at existing walls and fences as providing opportunities.

Wall and fencing materials and styles are as unlimited as your creativity. I prefer styles that allow air circulation while creating the screen I need, such as board and batten fencing. Your garden will be more comfortable on hot days, and plants experience fewer disease problems when there is good air circulation. Concrete and baked clay blocks that have air spaces not only permit air circulation but interesting designs as well.

Arbors and trellises also lend practicality, beauty, and vertical, and overhead support to plants. They are important in the Enabling Garden because they support plants so that they climb *up to you* to tend, harvest, or appreciate. These vertical elements greatly increase the growing space available if you can't get down to the ground or have difficulty bending. They also provide overhead support for hanging baskets and can be designed to provide some shade for comfort and safety.

Arbors (sometimes referred to as pergolas) are generally overhead structures that create dappled shade. In the plant nursery they are referred to as lath houses, and they protect young or tender plants from harsh sunlight. In the garden they protect tender people. They are most commonly wood structures, but I have also seen brick columns and steel pipes used to support roofs made of wood, plastic, and fiberglass. Arbors, while attractive alone, are enhanced when planted with vines that provide additional cover and shade.

Trellises sometimes cover the sides of arbors. They are also supporting structures on their own or in combination with containers. They can be made from wood, pipe, wire, or any combination. Very attractive fences can be made with trellises between stronger supports. Once covered with plants, they provide screening. In the vegetable garden, a trellis of pipes or 4 x 4 posts sunk into the ground, with string, wire, or cable strung between, may be the answer to raising vining crops or even support on which to train dwarf fruit trees.

Give thought to the plants you plan to grow on vertical structures. Some, such as wisteria, require very strong supports. Annual morning glories, on the other hand, can be grown on lightweight plastic netting simply tacked to a fence or any other convenient vertical support.

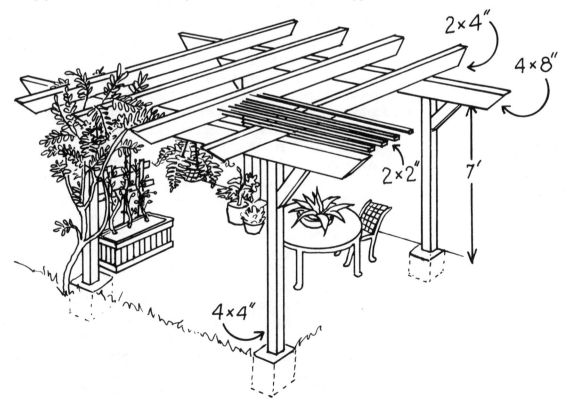

Vertical Gardening

Among the most important components of the Enabling Garden are the many vertical gardening methods that use fences, walls, arbors, and trellises to support plants or hang smaller plant containers. These often overlooked structures should be thought of as additional platforms to bring plants to a comfortable, accessible working height. They are also important in smaller gardens, where every square inch is critical. This is particularly true in the Enabling Garden, where expense can discourage you from paving, resulting in fewer, smaller accessible beds, even when a large yard space is available.

Vertical gardening can mean pole beans on netting, tomatoes on a stake, or a clematis vine on a trellis on either side of the garage door. Plants are brought closer to you for care, harvesting, or simply close appreciation of the intricacies of a blossom, stem, or leaf. The ideas that follow can increase the productive growing space in your Enabling Garden without taking up much ground surface space.

Smaller Containers Supporting small plant containers is the second easiest way to use vertical space available to you. (The easiest is simply to plant self-clinging or twining vining plants at ground level and let them climb within reach.) There are many outdoor bracket and shelving systems designed to attach to existing walls, balconies, railings, fences, and arbors, becoming platforms for placing small plant containers within easy reach. Many small containers are also made to be attached directly to walls, such as half, or wall, baskets made with one flat side. Some newer ones on the market are made in decorative clay and lightweight resin materials that look like stone, iron, and lead.

Vertical Wall Gardens

If you have the opportunity to build your own fences, or have walls and fences which can support additional weight, consider larger vertical wall gardens. These containers hold the unexposed soil surface perpendicular to the ground. Usually no more than 12 inches deep and whatever length and reachable height you want, they can be square, rectangular, or round.

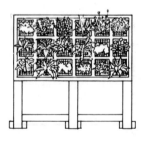

Vertical gardens hold a large amount of soil. Moisture is retained considerably longer than with most other container options because the soil is not exposed to air. The soil surface of the vertical wall garden is covered with 4- to 6-mil black plastic, then 1-inch-square, plastic-coated wire mesh, and finally a wood frame. With a large container, a trellis framework is attached with screws to delineate each plant area. With a smaller one, a "picture frame" of wood holds it all together. Screws are especially important because the soil should be changed once a year. In cold climates the planter must be emptied each fall so freezing, expanding soil doesn't push it apart.

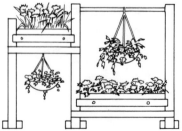

Any larger size, over 3 or 4 square feet, is quite heavy when filled with moist soil (see section on soil). It must be strongly supported either by the wall or fence itself or, best, by resting most of its weight on the ground or anchored off at the edge of paving using vertical supports. These containers are top heavy at accessible heights, so they must be securely anchored. They can be made or hung to allow knee clearance for the seated

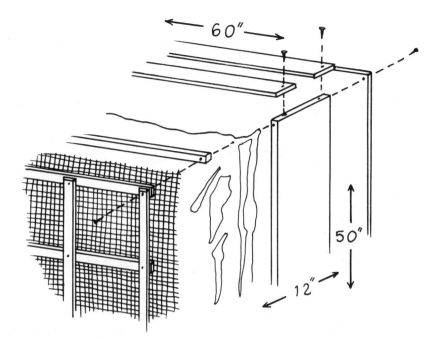

gardener. I have seen some on heavy-duty casters, which should be avoided, however, where the unanchored garden can be tipped over either by heavy winds or by the leaning gardener seeking support.

Once the boxes are constructed and filled with soil, cut holes 2 inches on a side into the wire. At each hole cut a cross or X into the black plastic with a sharp knife. Press a hole the same size as your transplant into the soil with your fingers. Carefully insert the root ball of the transplant and bring the black plastic around the stem. In just a few days, the plant will have rooted into the soil and will grow just fine.

The vertical wall garden is usually planted on one side only, but you can build it wider if both sides are accessible, accommodating the greater moisture and rooting volume needed by twice as many plants. A vertical wall oriented east to west could even have a shade garden on the north side and a sun garden on the south—now, that's diversity in a small space!

You must use transplants in vertical gardens rather than seeds because sprouting seeds would grow up through the container. The majority of shorter plants—even perennials in warmer areas—seem to do just fine planted sideways. You can plant virtually any dwarf (12 inches or less) annual and vegetable and any cascading plant. Avoid taller plants which will try to reorient themselves and grow up toward the sky.

Sort of sounds like a lot of work, and it is. These planters are quite complex to build, followed by annual assembly and disassembly in cold winter areas. But if you have the help to do these things, vertical wall gardens are very beautiful and productive. At the Chicago Botanic Garden Enabling Garden I have grown, in two 4 x 5-foot vertical wall gardens, with 40 square feet of growing space, a wide variety of spinach and lettuce in the spring, followed by summer annuals. In the best years, 60 pounds of salad greens were produced. Later in the season, visitors consistently remark about the virtually solid wall of flowers welcoming them into the garden, as these displays are prominently located at the entrance.

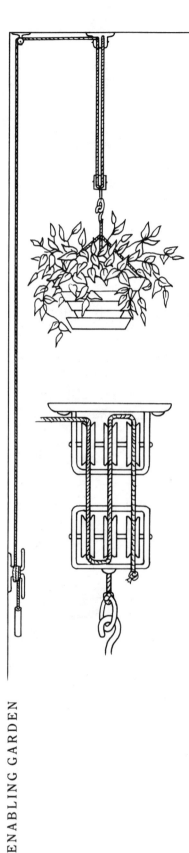

Another neat thing about these gardens is rabbits can't get at them, so you are assured a harvest. I have also experienced fewer insect problems. Perhaps they are fooled by the sideways planting. I'm not sure, but I'll count my blessings anyway.

Hanging Baskets If your Enabling Garden has such overhead structures as arbors or house eaves, you can hang baskets and other containers. Ropes and pulleys can lower a container for tending, then raise it again out of harm's way. With double or even triple pulleys, you can make a miniature block and tackle system, applying some of the things you learned in physics class to considerably reduce the strength necessary to raise and lower the basket. You can minimize accidents by tying a safety knot to become wedged in a pulley and stop a falling container, in the event control is lost.

While this chapter has not described every possible idea for raising the soil level to a comfortable working height you certainly have been given plenty of ideas about the containers and other structures you might like. The next step is to look at the tools and other equipment that can further your abilities in the garden. We have adapted the garden. Now it's time to adapt you.

Adapting You: *Selecting Tools and Equipment*

Up to now we have concentrated on adapting the garden by making it accessible to you. Now we'll begin to adapt *you* to be able to perform your planned gardening activities. Careful tool and equipment analysis and selection make gardening easier, while protecting you from unnecessary stress and injury.

Throughout my career I have been asked what tools and other equipment help the person with limited mobility garden more easily. This is perhaps the most difficult question to answer. While there are certainly many special tools and useful techniques, the unique abilities and limitations of the *individual,* as we learned in Chapter Two, become increasingly critical. Your general mobility, size, age, strength, balance, coordination, endurance, upper and lower reach limits, visual abilities, and many other factors are all important when addressing your equipment needs.

For example, if you cannot grasp a 1-pound soup can and hold it in front of you with your arm straight out, you probably need gripping aids, which support the wrist, or longer tools, which permit you to use two hands close to the body and maximize leverage. On the other hand, if you can hold a 3- to 5-pound weight straight out in front of you, many over-the-counter tools will be perfectly usable with minor changes, if any.

Another reason it is difficult to recommend specific types and brands is because while many effective tools are on the market today, many other recommended ones have disappeared from the stores and catalogs due to insufficient sales. Still others seem to survive, though they should have been thrown on the junkpile because they simply do not work. Ah, well . . . . Hopefully, as the powers that be come to understand that as a society we are aging, and that people with disabilities and people over 55 represent the two largest minority groups in this country, more effort will be put into designing products not only for the Enabling Garden but for easier daily living in general.

The good news is that many excellent enabling tools can be made by simply adapting the tools you purchase at most garden centers or hardware stores. The simple addition of extra handle padding or the replacement of an 8-inch handle on a hand cultivator with one that is twice as long, makes all the difference for some people in both comfort and access to gardening.

Additionally, many enabling tools are on the market that are specially designed for people with disabilities and older adults. These vary in quality and effectiveness, as do any other tools.

Esther U. (82), a retired judge, recommends using cafeteria trays when working on projects with several friends as a way of maintaining order on a chaotic table full of tools, soil, plants, and so on. Each person has his or her own set of materials in one place. Submitted by Joel Flagler, MFS, HTM, from New Jersey. (Author's note: I use a cafeteria tray with a 1-inch lip around the edge to carry stuff around. I've added anti-slip bathtub appliques on both the upper and lower surface also.)

KVCC KALAMAZOO VALLEY COMMUNITY COLLEGE LIBRARY

An associate of mine, an engineer by profession with an interest in easy-to-use gardening tools, once did a workshop with me where he actually made sense out of that dreaded (for me, anyway) high school physics class. He applied such principles as the fulcrum and the lever in discussing the design of garden tools and their resulting ease of use. Much of what he explained is applied throughout this chapter. Essentially, the best tools distribute effort and apply force the most efficiently.

*B*asic Enabling Tool Considerations

Tools are devices that extend your abilities. In the garden they extend your ability to work the soil and care for plants. When selecting tools for your needs, once again refer to the information you learned about yourself in Chapter Two and the structures and other plant containers you selected in Chapter Four. There are several basic things to remember when evaluating tools.

Lightweight tools are generally easier to use. Quality and durability may suffer with a garden fork half the weight of another model. If this simple weight criterion makes the tool usable, however, the choice is obvious. Some more expensive lines use fiberglass, aluminum, and composite handles, along with lighter metal blades that decrease weight yet maintain strength. Aluminum alloy blades for hand tools, such as trowels or cultivators, are much lighter than steel ones and don't rust if left out in the garden during a rain.

Longer handles can be up to 6 feet long on tools such as rakes, spades, and hoes. The standing gardener working on ground-level beds will benefit from increased leverage and less stooping. Tools with longer handles may also serve as walking sticks, enabling you to leave the cane behind while going out into your garden. Adding length to hand tools may bring more growing space within easier reach, especially for the person using a wheelchair and other seated gardeners.

A point of diminishing returns comes, though, in that the longer a handle, the heavier, and the more force it takes to both lift and use. For example, I have an extended-handle (48 inches long), two-cut-and-hold pruner that weighs about 2 pounds. It is one of my favorite tools for harvesting flowers, deadheading perennials, and other light pruning. It greatly extends my reach, and I have enough strength to hold it with one hand extended out to my side, giving me about a 6-foot maximum reach into a bed. After a very short time, however, my shoulder is exhausted because the work fulcrum (that is, the point at which a lever turns) is in the wrong place. Holding the tool in two hands closer to my body, I am able to use it much longer and much more comfortably.

Smaller blades and tool heads both reduce the overall weight of the tool and require less force to move through the soil and perform other gardening tasks. This is particularly noticeable with most long-handled hoes, spades, and rakes. You can create some of the most useful tools by combining the business ends of children's gardening tools with standard handles up to 72 inches long. The blades are about one-third to half the standard sizes and proportionately lighter and easier to use. The tool I use most in my ground-level garden is a thin-steel, 6 x 8, rectangular-bladed spade, with a rounded leading edge and a 60-inch wooden handle. It weighs only about 2½ pounds. My hoe-cultivator is a very lightweight single tine attached to a 60-inch handle, called a finger hoe. I also use a hoe with a small triangular blade 2 inches on a side, also attached to a 60-inch handle. I keep them all razor sharp with a nearby file, which makes them that much easier to use. At containers and raised beds, smaller blades are easier to work with, especially around plants close together.

Tool handles and grips must be given very careful consideration. Large-diameter handles are generally less tiresome to grip than smaller ones, but too large a grip can be equally uncomfortable. Your thumb and index finger should just begin to overlap when gripping a tool. Some comfortable tool handles are molded to fit a grasping hand.

The do-it-yourselfer can improve tool comfort by wrapping handles with foam rubber, taped in place with rubber electrical tape. Foam rubber tubes are manufactured for slipping over handles. They come in 6-foot lengths and are cut to the length you need—to slip over the longest spade handle or the shortest trowel. Any soft covering really makes a tool handle more comfortable. Some manufacturers are beginning to produce tools with a layer of foam rubber padding bonded to the usual wooden handle. You can find the best thickness for you by wrapping a handle with news-paper held in place with masking tape. Such experimenting will help you make better choices when buying permanent equipment.

Some people find the shorter, D-handled forks and spades easier to use. The handle allows two hands to grip side by side. More importantly, it allows you to add your weight, by leaning on the handle, to the downward force of pushing the tool into the soil. In the end, something as simple as slipping a bicycle handlebar grip over your favorite trowel may make all the difference in your being able to use the tool. All these materials not only add diameter and softness, being nonslip they are also easier to grip.

Two hands are better than one. If at all possible, select or make tools that enable you to use both hands held close to your body. With the added strength, leverage, and stability, you can perform basic tasks, such as cultivating, much longer without fatigue. Two-handed tools also distrib-ute force through more of your body and provide better control. This is particularly important when you're working from a seated position at a raised bed or wherever you must work to the side. Two hands on long-handled tools are critical for me to work my bermed beds at home. With-out the added strength and leverage provided by the second hand, I would quickly become exhausted, at which point whatever I'm doing would stop being fun.

Springs in tools that open and close, such as pruners and scissors, automatically return to an open setting. This is particularly useful when hand strength is weakened, and for repetitive tasks like cutting flowers.

Specific-purpose tools often take the greatest advantage of body position when they are used for the intended purpose. The scythe was one of the first special-purpose tools that was ergonomically designed. It allowed harvest of grain with both the wrists and the back in natural positions.

Polly Pageler, HTR, horticul-tural therapist at the Chicago Botanic Garden, uses parts of her person as measuring tools. "I use my finger be-tween the first and second knuckle to measure an inch for taking stem cuttings; my hand length and my forearm between wrist and elbow for measuring 6 inches and 1 foot spacing, respectively, for planting transplants. From my nose to my middle finger is approximately 1 yard for measuring lengths of string or ribbon."

Multiple-use tools, on the other hand, can vary in effectiveness, although the best of these are very useful. A Swiss Army knife, for example, is probably best used as a knife, even though it has a screwdriver, corkscrew, scissors, and so on.

Use your hands. Throughout my career I have repeatedly observed the one major factor that influences enabling tool selection: the soil level. If you raise the soil level to a working height, where you can get your hands in the soil, do it! Accomplishing this minimizes the need for adaptive equipment and tools. Get your hands dirty! With loose, easily worked soils (discussed in Chapter Six) and minimal hand strength, you should be able to do most everything with your hands alone. Working soil warmed by the summer sun feels great, too!

Use your hands whenever possible—it's good exercise. The next best argument for using your hands is that, for me, the biggest pain in using tools is carrying them around the garden. I use both hands to maneuver my wheelchair, so if I can't carry a tool on my lap, in the 3-gallon pail I carry between my legs, or in the bag that hangs behind my chair, I learn to get along without it. Pretty quickly, I was amazed at how few tools in my vast collection I really used much. I still use a pretty good variety for special, infrequent purposes, but I know the three to five I would grab if the garage were on fire!

*T*ypes of Enabling Tools

You now have a basic understanding of how tools work for you, bearing in mind overall weight, length, and handle diameter in relation to your abilities and garden plans. This section outlines various types of tools I have encountered and, in most cases, tried myself.

Most enabling tools fall into the following broad categories.

- Reaching aids
- Gripping aids
- Leverage aids
- Cutting aids
- Watering aids
- General aids

Each category contains a mixture of homemade and manufactured items. As before, measurements given are only general guidelines. If you buy an otherwise perfect tool with a 56-inch handle and only need 48 inches by all means cut it off. If the perfect tool blade comes with an unusable handle, change to a handle you like. Perhaps a small plate of metal welded to the top of a spade blade makes it more comfortable to apply force with your foot. The bottom line is to do your garden jobs as easily and comfortably as possible.

Again, always try to test out the tool before purchasing to determine its comfort, safety, and usefulness.

Reaching Aids

Reaching aids are simply tools that extend your normal ability to reach. If your hand and arm strength are relatively normal, or work with standard garden tools is possible with little difficulty, then only one simple modification is necessary: Select or make tools with **longer handles!** Adding a 24-inch handle to most hand tool blades will enable a wheelchair user or older gardener to easily reach the center of a raised bed 5 feet wide and work other large containers with one hand. A 48-inch handle enables two-handed use. For the standing gardener, longer handles up to 72 inches long extend reach and minimize stooping and bending at the waist.

Combining longer handles with **smaller, lightweight blades** greatly extends the comfort range of ground-level gardening. I accomplish virtually all of my traditional, ground-level gardening with my small spade and finger hoe, each with a 60-inch wooden handle. I also like my ingenious long-handled pruner, made by the ARS Tool Company (see Sources of Help), with interchangeable heads, including shears; a cut-and-hold pruner, which is invaluable for harvesting flowers, deadheading, and general light pruning; and a pruning saw. Its handle length can range from 2 to 10 feet.

These three tools are very durable and lightweight, but do require near-normal arm and hand strength. They enable me to tend beds up to 10 feet wide (I reach into the center from both sides). I'm sure as I get older, this range will narrow. Then I'll plant the center or rear of all the beds with lower maintenance shrubs and perennials.

A household reaching aid, designed for **grasping** cans, boxes, and bags off high shelves in the home, can retrieve items in the toolshed and reach small potted plants on the ground. Try to keep one in the toolshed so it is always handy. It employs a trigger grip: The harder you squeeze, the tighter the jaws of the tool close. Some models have a magnet on the end to retrieve small metal objects.

The Dramm and Gardena companies both manufacture aluminum **watering wands** that range between 18 to 36 inches. They come in even longer sizes, that when properly equipped (see Watering Aids), make watering much more reachable.

Several manufacturers produce tools with strong, lightweight handles and **interchangeable heads,** including rakes, hoes, and cultivators. Because of their light weight and versatility, they are worth a try.

Several types of long-handled, **cut-and-hold pruners** are available. They not only cut the flower stem, but grasp it for retrieval from the flower bed. They are also useful for removing dead blossoms, harvesting, and other "cut and hold" uses. The handles range from about 2 to 10 feet in professional models. As I said earlier, this is one of my favorite tools, although the trigger action to cut and grasp requires good hand strength. Pulling the trigger mechanism with all your fingers, rather than only your index, or trigger, finger, uses your hand strength more efficiently.

The firm-grip **weed puller**, with a 2- to 3-foot handle, has a sharpened end that digs and a trigger mechanism to uproot weeds. Once you loosen the weed, squeezing the trigger causes a bar to close over the weed for pulling and retrieval. This tool is fine in moist, well-amended soils, but difficult to use on weeds in grass. It is ineffective for dandelions and other taprooted weeds because it is difficult to remove all the root, which is necessary for control.

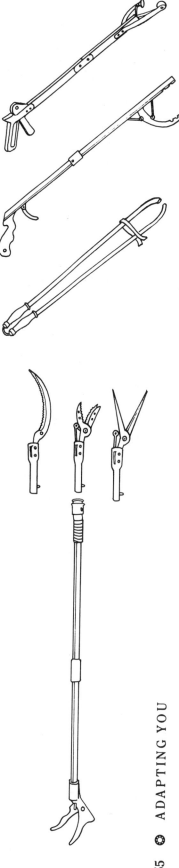

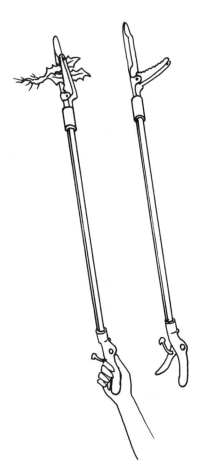

I also find the weed puller very useful for grasping small transplants and placing them in holes, dug with my finger hoe up to 5 feet away; I then cover them with the hoe. You have to practice to avoid crushing delicate plants, but you'll get the hang of it soon.

Avoid bending and stooping when planting vegetable seeds in rows by using any of several types of **plant row seeders**. The best ones are fully adjustable for planting small and large seeds at a variety of spacings. As you walk and push or pull the seeder, seeds are properly spaced along the row.

Plant row seeders are often recommended for people who use wheelchairs, but they are difficult. For one thing, you need two hands to maneuver the chair, so at best you can only plant a short section before moving up a few feet. Secondly, without paving, a wheelchair would sink in good vegetable garden soil. One idea is to lay planks for paths set on 28-inch centers, then run rows between your legs as you roll along. Furthermore, rows aren't the most efficient use of garden space, particularly if you have a mobility limitation.

What I use to plant seeds is a 48-inch length of ¾-inch PVC pipe. It is threaded at one end, with a removeable cap screwed on. I use this to punch holes or dig small furrows in prepared soil. Then I remove the cap, aim the pipe over a hole, and drop a seed down the pipe. Afterwards, I cover the seeds with the end of the pipe. The PVC pipe lets you plant seeds in virtually any spacing and configuration you want—within reach, anyway. This method works best with larger seeds, such as beans, peas, squash, and radishes. Smaller seeds, such as lettuce or carrots, work best if they are purchased pelleted (encased in a small ball of clay that makes the seed larger to work with).

Years ago I learned from someone how to make your own pelleted seeds. Slightly moisten tissue or toilet paper and tear off pieces about 1 or 2 inches square. Place a seed or two in the center, then gently roll the paper into a ball. Set your pelleted seeds aside to dry for a few hours, then go plant 'em. Sort of reminds me of spitballs way back when! This pelleting technique is also very useful for people who are visually impaired.

All of the above describe ways to help your reach. Comfortably increasing your reach greatly increases the area you can garden in all directions. Consider adapting some of the ideas in your own tool selection.

Gripping Aids

Gripping aids make all tools more comfortable. More importantly, if a gardener has weakened hands due to arthritis, neurological disease, or injury, holding tools at all may be difficult, if not impossible, without some kind of gripping aid. In addition, the gardener must be able not only to hold the tool but to apply enough force to do work with it. Therefore, the methods of making tools more comfortable to grasp and of supporting the hand range as wide as the abilities of gardeners.

Large-Diameter and Padded Handles Described at the beginning of this chapter as a basic tool consideration, simply building up a tool handle makes it more comfortable. Use resilient materials such as foam rubber, rubber tape, or grip tapes available in sports stores to build up a handle. This also improves handle traction, decreasing the strength needed simply to hold the tool without slipping. Padding minimizes vibration and pressure points. You can also purchase handles designed for crutches and canes, made of high-quality foam rubber, and slip them over the existing handles of most store-bought and homemade tools.

Gloves High-quality, pliable gloves protect sensitive skin, improve traction on tool handles, and keep hands warmer, which improves circulation and endurance. My favorite garden glove, available in any hardware store, is made of heavy, unbleached cotton fabric, with rubber or vinyl dots spaced evenly over the gripping surface. These dots greatly improve traction for both pushing my wheelchair around and using tools even when wet. They are less than $2 a pair. When the dots wear off, I wear the gloves one last time to change the oil or something equally gooey, then throw them away.

Molded Handle Conforms to the shape of the hand, as with finger indentations. Some handles connect to the blades at an optimum angle for best hand position.

You can add your own molded handle with plastic material, available from medical supply companies, that arrives soft in the package. Enclose the handle of your favorite tool in the plastic. While it's still soft, gently grasp the tool as you would in use, allow the plastic to conform to your grip, release it, and let it dry. The hardened plastic is still somewhat resilient, customized to *your* hand, and very comfortable to use. This allows you to have the best of both worlds: a larger, more comfortable handle, and one molded to your unique hand size and shape.

Utensil Holders Available at medical equipment suppliers, the utensil holder is for the person with little or no finger strength. A flexible, C-shaped plastic device, it slips over the hand between the thumb and index finger. A built-in pocket is positioned in the palm of the hand. There a spoon, fork, brush handle, toothbrush, paintbrush, or anything else with a small-diameter handle can be inserted and firmly held, eliminating the need for the fingers to grip the handle.

In the Enabling Garden, you can modify existing small tool handles to be accepted by the utensil holder. Most tool blades have metal that is embedded in the handle. Remove the existing handle and fit this metal piece into the holder. By leaving attached to these holders a basic set of tools, you will not have to change their heads.

A variation of this concept combines a holder with a wrist splint that attaches with Velcro. Besides holding tools, this device supports the wrist, which may be necessary if you have weakened forearm muscles that have difficulty moving the hand at the wrist.

Another holding system starts with Velcro straps attached by screws to the tool handle. A D-ring at the end of the strap enables the tool to be literally strapped to the hand. I am told this is better for some people than the typical utensil holder because it is more firmly secured to the hand. This may be used in combination with wrist supports, as well.

Sometimes all that is be necessary to help the person with little hand strength is to **wrap the hand and the tool handle together** with Velcro or an elastic bandage. Take care not to wrap them so tightly as to cut off circulation, which should be checked often.

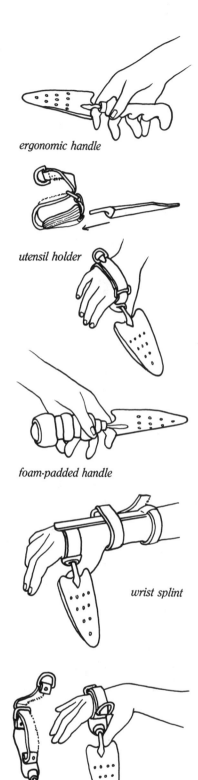

ergonomic handle

utensil holder

foam-padded handle

wrist splint

velcro strap on handle

(holes in trowel blade indicate inches for blind)

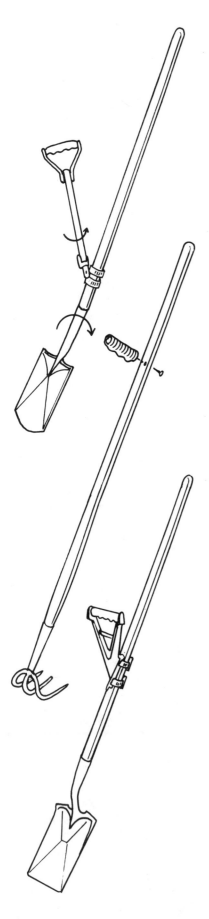

There are many degrees of hand, wrist, and forearm impairments, requiring aids ranging from the very simple to the rather complex. You and your medical consultant should be able to apply some of the techniques illustrated to enhance your ability to comfortably hold and use many kinds of tools in the garden.

Leverage Aids

You can use these helpers as supplements to any other enabling tool described in this chapter. Generally accessory handles, they provide added leverage or support your hands or arms so you can use tools more efficiently. Leverage aids may also transfer force from, say, weakened wrists to stronger shoulders. They can allow you to apply your strength to a better part of the tool, requiring less physical power to do the work.

There are two basic ways to improve leverage with tools. The first and simplest is to use **longer handles**. The longer the handle you can comfortably use, the more force, with less effort, you can apply to the business end of a shovel or spade. A variation of this principle is to simply attach an **accessory handle** at the position most comfortable to you. It reduces back and arm strain, as well as the need to bend at the waist. There are several types that attach with either clamps or screws. I would suggest you initially try a handle with clamps to determine the most comfortable position. Then you can drill screw holes for more permanent attachment. One 18-inch extension handle has a ball joint where it attaches to the tool, so it pivots easily.

The second basic approach to improving leverage is to use **handle-mounted devices** to essentially eliminate the need for a strong wrist. One such aid straps the tool handle to your forearm, with an additional handle, set at 90 degrees to the main tool handle, for your hand to grasp. This is very much the same principle used on special Lof-Stran crutches. The straps are best made of padded leather, or the flexible metal used on Lof-Stran crutches. In addition to added support and leverage, this method allows you to use the tool with one hand. Though more complex than some, this method really improves your ability to use tools longer without fatigue. It is especially good with leaf rakes, hoes, and cultivators.

A **tiller aid** attaches to garden forks, spades, and other long-handled digging tools. It provides a curved fulcrum for turning or lifting soil. Once you press a spade into the soil, for example, the tiller aid rests on the soil surface. By pulling the spade handle toward you, you make the aid serve as a fulcrum to lift the soil; then, by tipping the tool to the left or right, you turn the soil over.

Those who have tested the tiller aid say it takes a great deal of strain off the back and knees. It is, however, somewhat difficult to control exactly where you dump the soil. Also, the tiller aid is made from heavy gauge steel that adds considerable weight to the tool. If you still have the strength and mobility to turn ground-level garden soil, this aid can make it easier, but for me the best tiller aid is the high school kid down the street, who only requires a sharp spade, $5 per hour, and a few sandwiches.

Another important leverage aid for people with gripping problems is the increasingly popular **lever hardware** instead of household door-knobs. In the garden you can use it on gate closures, standard water faucet handles, and tool shed doors. It is much easier to use than door-knobs.

Almost as I wrote this section, a new set of hand tools has appeared, interestingly enough called **"Lever-Aides"** (see Sources of Help). They seem to be very durable and are designed to support weakened hands and wrists. The set includes a finger hoe, a cultivator, and a digging tool. A metal loop with padding rests on your forearm and accepts most of the resistance when you dig with the tool.

Improving leverage of a tool or transfering force to stronger parts of your body can greatly increase your garden abilities while decreasing risk factors. Ingenious devices are continually appearing which offer help and practicality. Take the time to seek them out.

Cutting Aids

Cutting aids are a group of tools for gardening tasks like harvesting cut flowers, removing dead blossoms from plants, and other pruning chores. Many medical supply companies offer household **cutting tools** for people with arthritis or weakened hands. These tools have many applications in the garden, and they may combine leverage and gripping aids in their design as cutters.

For general-purpose hand pruning, use high-quality, *sharp* **pruners**. The Felco series of pruners is excellent and readily available in most garden centers. They hold a sharp edge, have replacement parts by order, have comfortable handles, and, most importantly, have a spring that automatically reopens the tool. This last feature is a key one to look for in a cutting tool for your Enabling Garden.

Scissors with large openings in the handles permit several fingers to fit. This enables you to apply greater force to your work. A good friend with athritis very comfortably uses these for many household and garden chores. **Self-opening scissors** are available with various blade and handle sizes. A plastic band connected between the two handles springs back after compression. These scissors require much less strength, so you use them longer without fatigue. It helps that they are extremely lightweight and very sharp.

Some hand pruners use a ratchet action to gradually apply greater force to the branch being cut. I feel that if you can't easily cut with hand

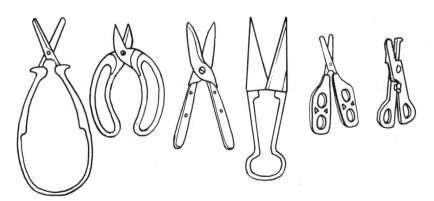

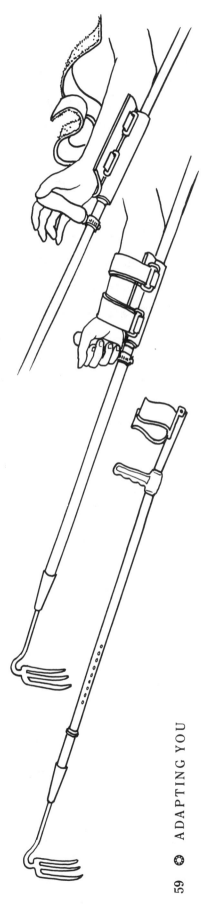

*Mary Rothert, my grand-
mother (84), uses a small,
lightweight wooden stool to
help her tend beds low to the
ground. She points out it is
important for the sitting platform to be rectangular rather
than round so there are
places to push off with the
hands. She also adds the
desired size depends on the
size of your rear end!*

pruners, you should move up to long-handled **loppers** or pruners, which enable you to apply much greater leverage to the job. Such tools require two hands and have handles from 18 to 36 inches long. I use these myself, as they extend my reach into the center of shrubs, help avoid thorns, and allow me to apply a great deal of leverage, easily cutting $1/2$- to 1-inch stems. Earlier I described long-handled pruners with interchangeable heads, which I find very useful in my garden.

All cutting tools can obviously be dangerous. You must keep them very sharp to be both effective and easier to use. Be careful about others using your tools, that the appropriate tool for the job is being handled properly. Always wear gloves for heavier pruning; they offer some protection for misplaced fingers. Handles brightly colored or painted with bands of contrasting colors, such as white and gray, help people with visual impairments avoid picking up tools from the wrong end. This technique applied to *all* tools helps you avoid losing or stepping on them, as well.

Watering Aids

Watering is one of the more difficult chores for me to perform in the garden. Hoses are heavy to carry, and once in position they always seem to be in my way because they run along the same walkways I use. They are impractical for me to roll up after each use, so they are left out and create a tripping hazard for others. Typically, hoses also require considerable hand strength to disconnect and reconnect. The essential high quality can be expensive. They never seem to be where they are needed; as I drag them to a new place, they inevitably seem to get caught on something, or I murder a favorite plant on the corner of a bed.

If you haven't gotten the idea, *I hate hoses!* They are, however, a necessary evil, and there are ways to minimize the effort needed to use them. Notice I said "minimize" not "eliminate." I have never seen a garden where a hose is not needed at one time or another.

Automatic irrigation can certainly eliminate the need for most hoses. Every major town should have a contractor who specializes in home irrigation systems that can cover most any situation. Coupling the spatial design with state-of-the-art household computer controls offers the ultimate in total garden watering. I have seen voice-activated computer controls that turned on not just lights, the television, and the stereo, but also any number of garden watering zones, automatically or on voice command, for any length of time. The thing even responded, "Yes master." It was an amazing system, and many newly built houses are wired for such electronic control. Its primary disadvantages are its complexity of installation and cost. Obviously, controls for an irrigation system can be totally manual, but installing pipes and even minimal controls may be beyond most budgets. If you have the resources, by all means go for it. An irrigation system, whether automatic or manual, can eliminate most of the major hassles of watering in your Enabling Garden.

I dream of my own system like the one above, but for now there are several strategies and tools that both make watering easier on me and conserve valuable water. Several are reflected in the type of gardening you do. The best watering aids are those that **lessen watering needs** in the first place:

1. Select plants native to your area, ones adapted to your climate, ones requiring watering only until established, if newly planted, or during extended drought. They will generally be less fussy, as well as more tolerant of insects and diseases.

2. Group plants in your garden according to their watering needs. Take advantage of garden locations naturally wetter or near downspouts for planting moisture-loving plants. On the flip side, use plants tolerant of drier soil in the high-and-dry spots, places hardest to get to, in your yard and smaller containers. There's always a place or two in the far corners of my yard I seem to neglect. That's where the tough, low-maintenance plants go.

3. Mulch! Mulch! Mulch! Preferably organic, which enriches the soil as it decays, mulch is the single best watering aid I know. Sure, you have to get the stuff, and you may need help spreading it. In the long run, though, you save a great deal of water, spend less time pulling weeds, and have better soil and healthier plants. Even a layer of leaves or grass clippings in a smaller container greatly reduces water loss.

4. Cut down on the number of smaller containers, which dry out quickly. Use larger containers, and keep any smaller ones in the shade.

5. Don't water till you have to. Sounds simple, but I think watering is overdone. Once plants are established, let a slight grayish leaf color or a little wilting tell you when watering is needed. Such watering encourages deep rooting and makes efficient use of the moisture already in the soil.

Use these five water savers, and you will spend less time watering in the first place. When these techniques must be supplemented, I have done the following to ease the pain.

First, I use top-quality, **reinforced rubber hoses**. They remain flexible when cold and resist kinking. The connecting hardware is the weakest point of any hose, so determine the total length you need to do the job and try to buy the hose in one length. Buy one 75-foot hose, rather than three 25-foot hoses connected to one another.

My rectangular ranch house has water faucets on all four sides, all of which are located at the rear of planting beds and other places inaccessible to me. In lieu of covering valuable garden space with paving, I connected heavy-duty, short (10 feet or so) **extension hoses** to reach my paths or other accessible places, where they connect to my other watering equipment. If you are fortunate enough to be able to install new faucets, they should be at an accessible height range of 18 to 30 inches. Place them by paving for both wheelchair access, if necessary, and to minimize mud and puddling water. Use **levers,** rather than round knobs, for on-off handles. Also, I have invested in enough hose on each side of the house to cover all the needs on that side. I leave it there, rather than move it from place to place.

At the end of each hose, I attach a high-quality, heavy-duty **brass shutoff valve**. My wife turns on the water for me at the house wall once in the spring and off again in the fall. (The water is also turned off at the wall outlet when we are away for extended trips.) The rest of the time, the hose stays pressurized, with total flow control maintained by the shutoff valve at the end. In order for this system to work, you must use high-quality hoses and leakproof fittings at all connections. I have used mine for 5 years with no problems, other than the one time I ran over a hose connection with the car and caused an irreparable slow leak.

Next I recommend heavy-duty, **brass snap connectors** at every connection point and on every watering tool. This makes the job of switching watering tools vastly easier. The Gardena Company makes a complete line of useful watering tools, including plastic snap connectors. These are lightweight and require less hand strength to use than the brass ones but not as durable if repeatedly dropped on hard surfaces.

My next most useful watering aids are black **rubber weeping, or soaker, hoses**. They are usually made from recycled tires and are very effective for large raised beds, ground-level beds, and any relatively inaccessible place. There are two minor drawbacks to soaker hoses. With your typical household water pressure, you cannot use more than 100 feet of soaker before the water pressure at the end becomes too low. There's a disparity between the water flow near the beginning, where pressure is higher, and that toward the end, where it diminishes. You can overcome this problem by reconnecting the source hose to shorter lengths of soaker hose laid out in the necessary spacing for your garden. I have done this in many of my beds, as shown. By snaking a soaker around in a larger raised bed, then connecting the water source hose to it, you can cover these areas as well.

The second soaker disadvantage is that to properly use it in an ornamental bed, you cover it with mulch, both to hide it, because it is ugly and distracting, and to further minimize evaporation, providing extra water conservation. Therefore, you have set up an invisible watering system, and that's where the problem comes in: I forget where I buried the soakers. Most of us avid gardeners are always trying new plants, rearranging them into different combinations, wedging that very last plant into the bed—and invariably hitting the soaker hoses. Things get further complicated when I create new beds or enlarge old ones, which requires redoing the whole hose arrangement. The hose can be left on the surface in the

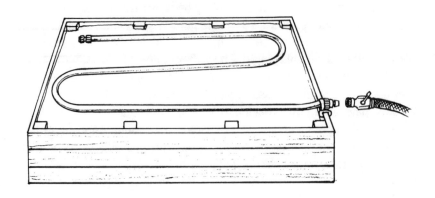

vegetable garden, though, where it is easily rearranged as crops are harvested or replanted.

The soaker disadvantages are minor compared with the less effective watering alternatives. Running one of these systems for several hours—early in the morning or at night, on a timer or manually—encourages deep soaking, which is important. Deeply water large trees by circling the soaker hose around the drip line (the area below the tree's canopy edge) and running it for several hours. Using a water timer helps take the guesswork out of this, too.

Despite their disadvantages, these soaker hoses have been a boon to me. Once installed, they make extremely efficient use of water, time, and effort.

An **overhead, oscillating sprinkler** is another good tool. It covers large areas of the garden and, in a rare extreme-drought situation, the lawn (I generally do not water my lawn, instead allowing it to go dormant during the peak heat of summer months). I have invested in two sprinklers, one for the front yard and one for the rear, and hide them in the shrubbery when not in use. They are fully adjustable, so I can accurately aim the water by sprinkler placement and controlling water pressure at the shutoff valve. I use these sprinklers only at night or very early in the morning to minimize evaporation, which could waste up to 30 percent of the water applied during a sunny, hot, dry, windy day.

The **long-handled watering wand** is a very useful watering and reaching aid, extending your ability to do overhead watering, and extending your reach into the center of beds and large containers. A wand is very handy for all hand-watering in the Enabling Garden. It is essential for spot-watering newly planted or transplanted trees and shrubs, which require more frequent watering than the surrounding established plants. By adjusting the flow to little more than a trickle and placing the wand near the base of the new plant for a few hours, it thoroughly soaks the root ball.

The two most common lines, made by the Dramm and Gardena companies, both rely on aluminum for their extended handles. The 30-inch long, 8-ounce Gardena wand has a built-in shutoff valve that is easily controlled by squeezing the handle, as well as a locked-on position for extended use without fatigue. It comes with a soaker nozzle in a plastic frame at the end. Dramm models range in length from 18 to 36 inches. One model bends at the top to make overhead watering of hanging baskets easier. Dramm's wands are usually marketed with a plastic soaker attachment that threads onto the end to break the force of the water.

The best head to use, however, is the heavy-duty, **all-aluminum head** used by professional growers, which can take repeated drops on concrete and other hard surfaces without breaking. I have three of the 24-inch, long-handled wands, each with a metal soaker nozzle and, of course, snap connectors. I leave one near each of my major garden areas; they are always handy, but hidden out of sight when not in use. Since my hoses have shutoff valves followed by the snap connectors, I have total control of not only on and off but also water volume with any tool I connect, whether it be a soaker hose, a sprinkler or a watering wand.

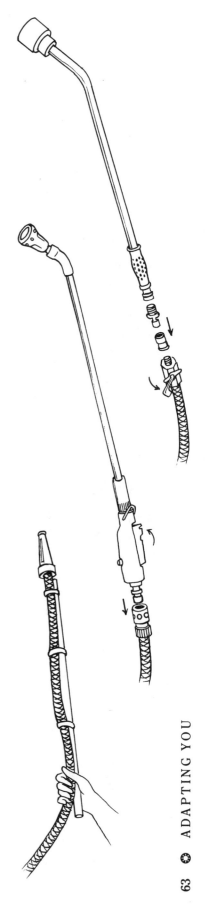

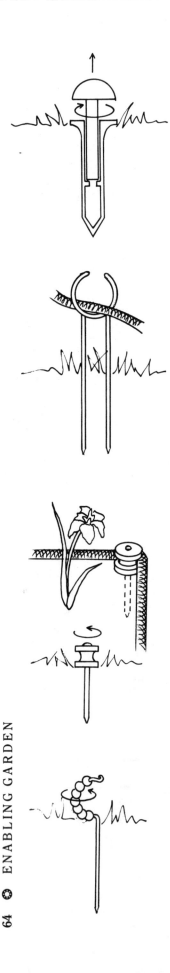

Because I use a wheelchair and need my hands to maneuver, I cannot easily carry things around the garden. I have therefore **duplicated frequently used equipment** and positioned it where I need it most. Besides minimizing moving the equipment around, this permits watering in several places at once. If you walk about and have good mobility, this would certainly not be necessary, and it isn't absolutely critical for me, either, but it sure is handy.

If you have greater mobility and free hands, you should consider the many types of **hose carts** on the market, made for transport and storage of hoses. Some models contain storage compartments for small tools. Hose carts range in features, durability, and cost—buy the best quality you can. The hose reels should turn easily (keeping in mind that the more hose you store on them the heavier the cart and the more force it will take to rewind the hose when fully extended). Start with shorter lengths of hose and move the cart to where it's needed. Try to find models that position the hose reel at the best height to minimize bending over or other awkward positions while reeling up the hose.

There are also many **wall-mounted hose reels** available. While you give up portability, you gain having the reel mounted at the best height for you. Look for high-quality models that swivel to permit easier positioning for unwinding and rewinding, turn easily, and don't leak.

The latest hose reels automatically rewind thanks to a spring-loaded action that tightens as you unwind the hose. A quick pull and the mechanism unwinds the hose. These are most effective when you use shorter, lighter hoses with few twists and turns in the route.

No garden should be without **hose guides**. There are several types on the market, ranging in both cost and effectiveness. Located at key points, they can prevent damage to plants and frustration. Be careful to position them not to be a trip hazard, or select brightly colored ones for greater visibility.

The mechanism that guides the hose is effective in most models, but the ground anchors may not be. The hose guide works when the spike or other anchoring device is wedged between paving stones or driven into heavier, unamended soils. In amended, loose, friable soil, however, the anchor spikes are usually too short and too easily pulled out of the soil. You must attach them to longer pieces of wood or pipe driven deep enough into the ground to be stable.

Some irrigation systems conserve water by using **drip emitters** and small tubing to deliver water directly to individual plants. The several variations on this theme would certainly be viable in many situations. A system is most easily set up in the vegetable garden or other places where plants are in rows and consistently spaced. The tubing must be taken up before tilling and reset each year, however, a chore preferably avoided in my case. It is very useful for automatically watering out-of-reach hanging baskets and other overhead containers.

The only other watering aids I have experienced are variations on the plain old **watering can**. Basic watering cans are fine if you are able to carry them. Remember, water weighs about 8 pounds per gallon. Lap trays help wheelchair users convey watering cans and many other items around the garden. Some plastic squeeze bottles with nozzles use a pump action to direct water to smaller or indoor plants without spilling. These are excellent for small spots, but they don't hold enough water for most outdoor jobs.

These ideas can make watering equipment choices easier. Most people with disabilities and older adults should be able to invest in some combination of watering ideas to make the inevitable task a lot easier on both you and your water bill. Once set up, hand-watering is very relaxing to most people, and one of the most popular chores in the gardening programs I have established. Running water seems to either have a calming effect or make you need to go to the bathroom. The former result is a very valuable stress management tool; the latter is good for your kidneys. It is amazing how therapeutic gardening can be!

*M*ore Enabling Equipment
Carrying Things Around the Garden

Those of us who use wheelchairs, walkers, crutches, and canes have a hard time carrying things around because our hands are used for mobility. Depending on your overall mobility, there are several ways you can transport tools, plants, and other stuff around your garden. The more restricted your mobility is, the more essential it is to ease the load by careful selection of proper tools in the first place and rigs for easily carrying them around. Consider stationing duplicate sets of often used tools where they are needed most. A small hand trowel or cultivator tucked away in the raised bed, on the patio, or out in the vegetable garden is a favorite trick. Of course, you would not leave sharp cutting tools lying around.

A **garden cart** is a better alternative to the wheelbarrow because it uses two or more wheels, giving more stationary stability and improved balance when moving a load around the garden. Some even fold up for easy storage. One two-wheeled cart called the Easy Wheeler is especially lightweight. It has a low center of gravity and is easily maneuvered. You can even use it with only one hand. Any such cart is a great aid to the active gardener. It not only carries heavier materials, but it helps avoid unnecessary trips when loaded with all the tools and other stuff you need, saving your energy for more important things.

A child's **four-wheeled wagon** is an excellent way to carry things around. It is usually low to the ground, so pretty stable. You could even carry a cushion or removable seating to make the wagon serve as a portable bench.

A well-designed **garden apron or a tool belt** with plenty of pockets helps you move stuff around the garden and keep your hands free. You can carry long-handled tools in a **crutch and cane holder** made to attach to a wheelchair. Various trays attach to the wheelchair or, with padding, conform to your lap; use such a **lap board** to transport small tools, pots, and watering cans. Its only disadvantage is that you cannot bend over when it's in place. I also use a 2- to 3-gallon plastic pail, sitting on my wheelchair footrests between my feet, to move small tools, plants, and

Sally Morgan works with a wide variety of people with disabilities and older adults at a United Cerebral Palsy horticultural therapy program in Pennsylvania. She recommends using moisture meters, especially those with colors along with numbers. Numbers may be difficult to read for some people, but colors are readily seen and understood. This helps prevent under- and overwatering. She goes on to say weeds are difficult to separate from perennials in the spring. Try loosely tying a string or ribbon around plants to be saved.

other things. **Cup or soda can holders,** designed to hang on wheelchair armrests, will hold a few hand tools just as easily as beverages.

Assorted bags are designed for hanging on walkers, certain types of canes, and wheelchairs. Those made of netted material and slung below the seat are very handy, as are those that hang on the back of the chair like a backpack.

The **Easy Gripper** looks like a pooper scooper, but it is essentially a giant, long-handled tweezer, letting you pick up debris without bending and deposit it into a cart or on the compost heap.

General Garden Helpers

There are literally hundreds of other products for household and garden use available from vendors listed in the resource section of this book, that make life easier in the Enabling Garden. I've described a few in the following.

If you have some ability to get up and down from the ground, **kneeling cushions and strap-on knee pads** greatly increase comfort and protect your knee joints. The "E-Z Kneeler," useful for getting up from your knees, can be flipped over to serve as a sitting bench. Any lightweight, short stool or bench may be helpful. Bathtub benches work very well in the garden. Some of these are height-adjustable via pins in the legs.

A **hand seeder** is good for working with small seeds that are difficult to see, handle, and sow. It has adjustable openings that dispense individual seeds, minimizing overseeding. It may be an excellent tool if you lack fingertip sensitivity.

Cordless electric tools, such as weed whackers, hedge clippers, and hand-held shears, are safer and easier than power tools with cords. Their power aids weaker muscles, but it also makes them potentially harmful if carelessly used. Cordless sprayers eliminate hand-pumping and the need for strong trigger fingers. I have also just learned of a rechargeable electric lawnmower: lightweight, quiet, less polluting than gas-powered mowers, and great for smaller areas.

Sprayers can be as simple as the small trigger sprayers that commonly mist plants and treat insect and disease problems. They require strong trigger fingers. The next best sprayer also holds a quart or less but relies on a hand pump to be pressurized. It also uses a trigger action to spray. The best has a locked position that stays open until it is released. The next step up in quality is the cordless electric sprayer, which uses batteries or is rechargeable. It requires the least effort of all. For larger jobs, the hand pump pressurized kinds, holding 1 to 2 gallons, works well but is heavy and difficult to carry around. I feel the best is the backpack type, with straps to carry just like a backpack. It has a pump to pressurize and holds up to 3 gallons.

Nonslip pads, approximately ¼-inch thick, soft, flexible rubber cut into either circles or rectangles, are put under dishes or placemats to prevent pots, pans, and dishes from slipping around. These are a great gardening help, especially if you are able to use only one hand. They also hold flowerpots and plant trays without slipping.

You can adapt a good set of **barbeque tools** for many uses. The sharp tines on the fork can be bent and dulled to serve as a cultivator for closely spaced plants in containers and raised beds. (It also makes a wonderful backscratcher.) Tongs can pick up dropped lightweight items or help position a transplant. The flipper spatula, cut and bent to an appropriate angle, can serve as a hoe. You can modify any of the handles to be more comfortable.

The major point with all these tools is to keep your eyes open to see what might be adapted for some purpose in your garden.

Tool Storage and Greenhouses

Your **tool shed** should be carefully designed, with all equipment within easy reach. Doors should be lightweight and a minimum of 30 inches wide. For a wheelchair user, sliding doors may be easier to use than hinged doors. The shed itself must permit a wheelchair to turn around. Otherwise, consider a linear design with doors at either end, allowing a wheelchair user to roll straight through, with tools handily arranged on both sides. The main point is to keep the materials and equipment you need readily available.

A waterproof **storage locker** hidden in some convenient place out in the garden may be all you need. You can also create a storage compartment under a bench, with the seat hinged to form the lid. This concept can also be incorporated into deck seating and benches combined with plant containers (described in Chapter Four).

A **greenhouse,** if you are fortunate enough to have one, can readily be adapted for access. Doors should be at least 30 inches wide and sliding, if possible. The bottom track must be sunken level with the surrounding pavement. Better yet, hang the door on a track to eliminate entirely the bottom track, which tends to collect debris, interfering with smooth opening and closing and creating a tripping hazard.

The floors must have the essential qualities described in Chapter Three—good drainage, traction, firmness, and levelness. Loose or interlocking pavers and bricks installed in sand offers the best drainage, although concrete can be used with a floor drain. Aisles should be roomy enough to accommodate a wheelchair's turning radius. However, I would not mind the one-way traffic or a narrower aisle in order to gain extra growing space. If two or more people must use the greenhouse, aisles must be appropriately wider. The fully ambulatory gardener can have narrower aisles.

Benches must be at an accessible height. At least 27 inches clearance is needed for wheelchair users, with minimum support posts to get in the way. Bench height can be whatever is comfortable for you, though. Their width is governed by your reach, as wide as possible to maximize growing space. If seated, about 24 inches is accessible from one side; the standing gardener should manage 30 inches or so. I found the stairstep structure described in Chapter Four an excellent way to display smaller pots in greenhouses.

Water spigots, lights, and any automated controls must be located in an obvious, convenient place, each easily identified and labeled in large letters, or Braille, if necessary.

✤

Jean Gillooly, HTR, offers the following tips for blind gardeners she learned from gardeners at the Cleveland Society for the Blind. A blind person can use his or her hands to find the center of a 4-inch pot when transplanting small plants. Place the index fingers, bent at the second joint, on opposite sides of the pot. Where the fingertips meet is the spot where the plant goes. When leading a blind person, place his or her right hand just above your bent left elbow. You can guide him gently behind you when approaching a doorway. Walk normally, describing the situation 6 to 10 feet ahead. A blind person can plant marker plants, such as dusty miller, in the garden to locate points where types of flowers or vegetables change.

for chapter 5:

✤

Using these basic considerations, you can adapt most any greenhouse or shed design for your Enabling Garden. Consult books and greenhouse builders to get the most from these valuable garden assets.

Helpers for the Visually Impaired

Getting around and using your Enabling Garden poses special challenges if you are visually impaired or blind. The following tips can help.

- ✪ A path should have a definite beginning and end.
- ✪ While edging isn't a necessary guide for a cane user, a textural change between the edge of a path and its surroundings is essential, for example, gravel to grass, bricks to planting bed, wood to bricks.
- ✪ Avoid sharp edges on all structures and containers.
- ✪ Use wind chimes or a small, noisy fountain as an orientation feature.
- ✪ Use tools with brightly colored handles to prevent loss and accidential grasping of sharp blades.
- ✪ A wooden planting board with equally spaced notches or a rope with spaced knots will help space plants evenly.
- ✪ Use brightly colored plants, ones with visual textural contrast, and those that emphasize tactile (touch) and scent qualities. Blind gardeners have said, however, not to use too many scented plants together, such as a collection of scented geraniums, because their different scents tend to run together into an inseparable "mush."
- ✪ Avoid vegetable plants whose fruit is picked green, which can be difficult to distinguish against green foliage. Try purple podded or wax bush beans, instead of the typical green beans.
- ✪ Last, but not least, talk with other gardeners who are blind or visually impaired for their tips. Also, many schools for people with visual impairments have gardening programs and would be happy to share their successes with you.

*E*nabling Tool Sources and Selection

In the final analysis, once you have raised the soil to a comfortable working height through the many ideas in Chapter Four, the need for special tools is minimal, unless weakened grip, hands, or wrists are a problem. Beyond reaching aids, I personally use little other specialized equipment.

If the need is there, though, many of these tools come and go on the market. You may have to make many yourself, or have them made for you, as ideas emerge. Talk to other gardeners; see what they use and where they got it. Equipment from medical supply companies, designed for people with disabilities and older adults, can be applied to garden tasks requiring special tools and equipment. In fact, catalogs consistently contain the latest in this type of equipment; I always get gardening ideas when I page through one.

Seek out horticultural therapy programs through the resources at the end of this book. They have tools and other innovations you can try out before making purchases. Rehabilitation hospitals are also sources of information on household enabling equipment, much of which you can apply to your garden. Many older adult day treatment and centers have gardening programs that are excellent sources of ideas, as do local independent living centers, which provide many services to people with disabilities. I learn the most from interactions with other disabled and older gardeners. Whether they be across the backyard fence or across the country, there are hundreds of thousands of gardeners who use special equipment and techniques, and who would be honored to share their special tricks to overcome some limitation, enhance some ability, and achieve continued success in the garden.

I want to reemphasize that you should always try to use a tool before you purchase it. Feel its balance and weight, go through the motions of using it in the garden, no matter how crazy you look, and buy the best quality tool you can afford. Tools last a lifetime if they are high quality to begin with and well cared for. Proper selection of reach extenders and leverage aids may also delay or even negate the need for a complex garden structure.

The best tool of all is between your ears. Life with a mobility impairment is a constant challenge in adaptation—we're masters at it. Applying your creative abilities in your Enabling Garden will overcome many barriers.

6

Adapting the Plants:
Plant Selection

Sandra Foreman, HTM, shares a suggestion from Trudy (79): Trudy has difficulty seeing small seeds, so she dusts them with flour.

This chapter emphasizes "adapting" plant materials by selecting those you enjoy growing and eating, whose maintenance requirements are in accordance with your abilities, and which challenge your growing skills.

If there are two things that are not in short supply, they are books and opinions on gardening. Any bookstore or library has a selection. Particularly excellent are libraries at public gardens, which will specialize in botany and horticulture. In addition, every gardener has his or her favorite plants, garden design, and techniques, and is always willing to share them with friends and fellow gardeners, whether they want them or not. There are also many fine gardening shows on public and cable television; many are later released on videotape, available at video stores and general and horticultural libraries. The point is, no matter where you live or move in the country—or the world—you can tap into local resources about your favorite hobby.

My gardening experiences are limited to the Midwest, so I can recommend few specifics about plants in the tropics or the far north. However, Chicago certainly is one of the more challenging places for gardening, so many principles will apply to your area, with local resources providing the details. This chapter reviews several types of plants and how they relate to the Enabling Garden, with a few of my favorites in each category.

Actually, in the Enabling Garden, growing the plants is the easy part and the most fun. Your local climate and your ability to do maintenance will, to a great extent, dictate what you should attempt to grow, but I have never seen a situation where that list is very short. In addition, there will always be that new rarity to seek out.

When selecting plants for your Enabling Garden, bear in mind the following criteria that apply to any general category of plants.

Emphasize plants with interesting color, scent, texture, and form. This basic principle is particularly important in the Enabling Garden, where certain senses may be impaired. Selecting plants with extremes in the above qualities will help overcome limitations or compensate through other senses. For example, bright, bold color contrasts may be better seen and enjoyed than pastel colors by people with visual impairments.

Strong visual or tactile (touch) contrasts in texture, such as a combination of ferns (soft) and hostas (coarse), are interesting to the eye, as annual strawflowers and perennial lamb's ears are stimulating to touch. Even thorns are okay, up to a point.

While I do not have any sensory limitations, I consider scent one of my most important plant selection criteria. Locate a lilac or viburnum shrub near a window, where the casual breeze draws the flowers' fragrance into your house. Grow any of the hundreds of varieties of herbs and spices, which, both fresh and dried, stimulate both the nose and the tongue. Even include plants that release their scents in the evening or at night, such as the moonvine and some lilies. These are only a few ways of incorporating scent into the garden.

Scent triggers memories and is said to be the most evocative of sensory stimuli. One of my most vivid memories as a young two- or three-year-old kid was visiting my great-grandfather's farm and watching him pick and cut open a perfectly ripe honeydew melon—that fragrance is unmatched. I don't remember much else about him, but I will never forget his sharing that melon with me. And to this day, whenever I first cut open one of those melons, I think of him.

Contrasts of form are also important for interest and visibility. On a large scale, the low, horizontal branching pattern of a pagoda dogwood presents a bold contrast to vertical evergreens. On a smaller scale, low, mounding perennial geraniums give a strong form contrast to vertical ornamental grasses.

Even without combinations of plants, you can create interest with individual specimens of plants with strong sensory characteristics.

Select plants based on the amount of maintenance you can perform. Some plants naturally grow and look better with dead blossoms removed. Some shrubs flower only on new wood, so you must continually prune them to encourage new growth. Vegetables obviously require you to stay on top of harvesting. Many such plant-related chores take time and effort.

If you are both *able* and *willing,* you can plan your garden to be a full-time job. Otherwise, you have to scale back the work required to your time and physical abilities. When I plan gardening projects for a hospital, for example, I have many gardeners eager to stay involved, so I choose plants that need pinching back, frequent harvesting, or deadheading (removing spent blossoms). At home it's another story. I don't mind working in the garden for exercise and therapy, but I work more than full-time. If I can't keep my garden looking good with just an hour every couple of days, it's too much, and I'll replace some annual beds with low-maintenance shrubs. I'll do the same as I get older, when I won't have the strength or endurance to perform at my current level.

Plant selection has a great impact on the amount of work you must— or want—to do. Many reference books list plants requiring lower maintenance. I would view roses as a high maintenance plant and a cactus as a comparatively low-maintenance plant. Get the idea?

Knowing what size trees and shrubs ultimately become is very important. Don't, for example, put a plant so near a walkway that it will later require frequent pruning to keep from encroaching on the path. Don't create unnecessary work!

Low-maintenance plants are also important in areas of your yard that are not easily accessible. Let's face it: I can't get my wheelchair to *every* place in my yard, but that certainly doesn't mean I can't incorporate such areas into my garden somehow. I use lower maintenance trees and shrubs as interesting things to cover the ground in these areas. I simply don't have to get at them very often. I am also interested in dwarf and compact plants of all kinds because they stay in bounds without pruning. By virtue of their smaller sizes, they also allow me to use more varieties while using less space in my garden.

Use plants with four-season interest. With a mobility impairment, you must look toward your immediate surroundings for important environmental satisfaction. Therefore, selecting plants that offer something different and interesting throughout the year is very important, particularly in areas with long, cold winters. Here in Chicago, a plant's winter character is often more important than its look in the summer.

One of my favorite plants for illustrating this point is the Washington hawthorn (*Crataegus phaenopyrum*). This 20- to 30-foot tree flowers late in the spring, after most shrubs and other trees; it has attractive, glossy, green leaves through the summer; gives you bright orange to red fall color; and upon leaf drop, bright orange-red fruit is revealed, which persists through most of the winter, providing food for birds. Its vase-shaped form, with dense horizontal branching, often catches the snow. This, in combination with the bright fruit, is one of my favorite winter scenes. To cap it off, the plant is tough as nails and is a favorite of nest building birds. That's long-season interest!

Many annuals and perennials offer attractive seedheads, earth tone colors, and textures for the winter landscape if left standing rather than being cut down in the fall. These special plants give a great deal of satisfaction to the enabling gardener when the garden must be viewed from indoors.

Select plants that extend the growing season in your area. One of my favorite gardening challenges is to find plants which flower or are otherwise effective at the extremes of the growing season. The increasingly popular ornamental kale stays colorful into early December in years with mild falls, but is usually reliable through Thanksgiving. I also planted snowdrops bulbs at the base of my south-facing porch wall, so I've got some color as early as the end of January. Other early spring bulbs, such as early-flowering perennials as hellebores, and shrubs like witch hazel bloom in late March, bringing welcome color following a drab, cold winter. Another favorite group is the many late summer- and fall-blooming plants, such as snakeroot (*Cimicifuga* spp.), asters, or toad lilies (*Tricyrtis* spp.), which challenge the frosts of fall, as well. You can plant many vegetables with the first warming of the soil, while you can harvest others from under the first snows. This characteristic of plants is one of the best therapies the garden offers me; I can look at the garden just about any time of the year and find something of interest. Monitoring day-to-day changes and seasonal rhythms throughout the year is an important source of enjoyment for most gardeners.

Include plants that attract birds, butterflies, and other wildlife. There is something very exciting about planting something known to attract butterflies, then seeing the first tiger swallowtail or monarch use the plant for a nectar stop. Strategically designing plantings to provide food, cover, and nesting sites for birds, then seeing them used, is a special thrill. Rabbits and deer can indeed create the thrill of knowing you've created an enjoyable habitat for nature's creatures. They can also generate very negative emotions in you, however, when they get to your "just about ready" garden lettuce even as you were going to sleep anticipating fresh salad for *your* lunch the next day.

For the most part, however, animal intrusions into the garden are positive. Local cooperative extension offices and public gardens have information on plants not attractive to your local problem animals, as well as lists of plants that will attract beneficial wildlife.

Include edible landscaping. Edible landscape plants form a broad category. Beyond the obvious edibles found in the vegetable garden, you can select many other plants that offer something to eat. Edibility is perhaps not the most important criterion for plant selection, but some non-traditional options for raising food in the garden require lower maintenance. For example, if you need a medium-sized shrub, why not try a dwarf apple, peach, cherry, or nectarine tree? These dwarf trees offer easily harvested fruit and are very productive. Blueberries, gooseberries, raspberries, and currants are among the worthwhile small, fruiting shrubs. In warmer areas, the choice of tropical fruits is enviously nearly endless.

Many perennial vegetables and fruits—including artichoke, rhubarb, asparagus, and strawberries—once properly planted, provide harvests for many, many years. Beyond the obvious food plants, many of our commonly used landscape plants also offer edible harvests, as long as we beat the birds and other wildlife to them. Juneberry, hickory, walnut, pecan, and persimmon trees offer big harvests for the taking. Where a vine is needed, try grapes or kiwifruit.

There is certainly more care involved with most of these crops besides just planting them and sitting back till harvest time, but at least they don't require planting every year. An initial investment in acquiring the plant, preparing the soil, and planting pays off for a long time.

Select plants that are indigenous to your area or varieties, hybrids, and cultivars of native plants. Indigenous plants are best adapted genetically to local soil conditions and climate extremes. Many exceptions to this rule are found in the hundreds of excellent garden plants that are not native but do come from similar climates. So-called natives, however, are more resistant to local pest and disease problems and better adapted to your growing conditions, so they should generally be more reliable than others.

Select plants appropriate for containers and raised beds. This is especially important in two repects, garden accessibility and plant hardiness. Depending on the size of the container, you can grow virtually any plant from the smallest alpine plant to a large tree. It *is* important to consider the container's added height when a fragrant rose 3 feet tall flowers in a raised bed 2 feet high. The blossoms 5 feet high will be beyond of the nose of the seated gardener. Likewise for growing corn and tomatoes. You must remember that the plants in your Enabling Garden must not exceed your reach limits if they require tending, harvesting, and so on. Low-maintenance trees, shrubs, and vines can certainly be selected that require minimal attention, and the fact that they are largely out of reach may not be important.

Secondly, plants grown in aboveground containers, even large raised beds, are more exposed to the rigors of winter freezeing and thawing. They are also generally colder than well-mulched, snow-covered, ground-level beds, simply because they are more exposed. Therefore, a plant that would normally survive a winter in your area may be killed in a container. Studies are lacking on this, but a good rule of thumb to follow is to use container plants that will survive winters at least one climatic zone colder than your area, according to the U.S.D.A. Hardiness Zone Map. This will help prevent disappointment following a particularly cold winter. Of course, those of you in warm areas of the country can thumb your nose at this problem and grow virtually anything you wish.

When selecting permanent and perennial plants, be sure they are hardy to your area. You can use the U.S.D.A. Hardiness Zone Map as a guide, indicating average minimal temperatures. The hardiness of most plants is classified by this or similar systems. However, many other factors besides cold tolerance affect plant hardiness. Summer heat is a known limiting factor for some plants. Moisture, soil type, wind exposure, winter snow cover (which serves as a protective mulch), the plant's native climate, exposure to winter sun—all affect plant health and vigor and, hence, tolerance for weather extremes. A person who is healthy and vigorous is more tolerant to weather extremes and other forms of stress than one with a vitamin deficiency or is otherwise ill; plants similarly have multiple hardiness factors.

So, use hardiness zone maps only as guidelines. I encourage you to challenge the rules. For example, Chinese dogwood (*Cornus kousa*) is regarded as a Zone 6 plant. I planted one in my yard, within Zone 5, yet it has lived five years now without injury. I know that if the temperature drops to 25 below zero, I will get some serious dieback, but the plant gives such spectacular and longlasting fall color, it's worth the risk. We get to 25 below zero only about once every ten years, so why not enjoy the plant now? I feel the same about perennials: If I can enjoy a plant for a few years before a bad winter takes it out, it is worth the experience particularly if I can take advantage of a particular microclimate in my yard that enhances its chances.

Consider toxicity of plants when planning the garden. You must consider this factor if you or a visitor, such as a child or an older adult with memory loss or Alzheimer's disease, might accidentally eat the wrong thing. In general, I feel the concern given this in the literature is overblown. Don't get me wrong: There are poisonous compounds, especially in many tropical plants, that, in concentrated form or if a large enough volume is eaten, will make a person sick. Serious poisonings from eating plants are fortunately extremely rare. This doesn't mean you should surround yourself with a collection of deadly plants, only that you could temper your concerns.

Besides oral toxicity, you should be aware of skin irritations and allergies stimulated by contact with various plants. Such reactions may be very individualized, so be observant and cull out any plants that cause you or any family member problems. The *AMA Handbook of Poisonous and Injurious Plants* is the best guide, with application across the country. Simply be aware that some people react to some plants more than others. You should take precautions when working alongside others who may have adverse reactions either on their own or because of medications that enhance sensitivity to toxic plants.

The bottom line is grow what you want to grow. You will be successful if the plants you select are compatible with your site and ability to provide care—but that's what gardening is all about!

*E*nabling Garden Soil

Before embarking on acquiring all the wonderful plants you have picked out, you must consider what you will plant them in—namely, the soil. Every gardener knows the relationship of good, healthy soil to a good, healthy garden. Without a medium that physically supports the plants, provides essential nutrients, air, and water, you may as well stick to plastic plants and garden statuary, which are certainly easy to care for, but not very stimulating. The time, effort, and money invested in creating good garden soil will pay off immensely not only in plant health and vigor, but also in your enjoyment of the garden.

In the Enabling Garden, you are fortunate because a well-amended soil that is good for plants is going to provide the qualities you require as well. There are two essential characteristics Enabling Garden soil needs: It must be loose, friable, and therefore **easily worked** by weakened hands, perhaps. Tool blades must easily penetrate, and the soil must be easily tilled, if necessary. This quality will make all digging, transplanting, weeding, and planting much easier. Second, the soil must have good **moisture retention,** particularly those soils used in smaller containers. This quality is necessary to minimize the need to water. The good news is that these qualities benefit the growth of most plants as well.

Without going into all of the science of soils, the key to improving just about any existing ground-level suburban, urban, or other soil that has been disturbed through construction activity is **organic matter**. Organic matter improves aeration, drainage, and moisture-holding capacity, and makes nutrients available to plants as it decays. Perhaps most importantly, it encourages life in the soil. Bacteria, fungi, earthworms, and insects are important parts of the natural soil ecosystem. These organisms are the decomposers that break down organic matter and release nutrients to plants. Many plants have even evolved symbiosis with various soil bacteria and fungi, whose activities are necessary for the general health of the plant.

Bed Preparation

When preparing new planting beds, incorporate 4 to 6 inches of organic matter, such as leaves, grass clippings, compost, wood chips, chipped landscape waste, recycled Christmas trees, straw, shredded bark, and stable sweepings, into the top 2 to 3 inches of existing soil. First, however, it is important to roughly turn over the existing soil to a depth of one spade blade, or about 10 inches. Leave this soil in rough clods. Then lay the organic matter over the top and mix it into the top 2 to 3 inches of soil. It is very important not to bury organic matter too deeply, as it will decompose differently without air and create an environment toxic to plants. Nature always maintains most of the raw organic matter in the top few inches of soil, where most of the soil microorganisms live. This mixing does not need to be thorough, as long as soil and organic matter make good contact. If possible, top this all off with another couple of inches of organic matter as a mulch, and keep the bed fallow (idle) for a year so the mix has time to cook down into the best soil you have ever had. The final grade will be 8 to 10 inches above the surrounding soil, better drained, healthier, *and* easier to reach.

Working organic matter into existing beds around shrubs, trees, and perennials is also of benefit. You should take care, however, not to damage roots. Do not turn the existing soil over deeply; instead, carefully scratch organic matter in and around the existing plants. Finally, cover the soil between plants with 2 to 4 inches of organic matter mulch. *Always* cover exposed soil with plants or organic mulches to discourage erosion, conserve moisture, hold down weeds, add nutrients, and serve as basic organic matter replacement.

For raised beds and other large containers, a very satisfactory soil can be mixed from equal parts, by volume, of sharp sand, any commercial topsoil, and peat moss or compost. Organic matter will need to be renewed annually, as it decays and the soil volume shrinks.

One final important point is that once you have prepared soil, keep it light and fluffy by staying out of the beds. Use stepping stones, long-handled tools for reaching and adequate access paths—but don't compact the soil. Second, avoid further tilling or turning the soil, other than perhaps that in the vegetable garden. Soil with plenty of organic matter establishes a well-drained, porous structure that is great for plants. Better yet, you can easily pull weeds and dig holes in it. Tilling, besides being hard work best avoided, destroys this structure. So stay out of the beds!

Soilless Mixes

For smaller pots, hanging baskets, and other containers, I recommend commercially prepared soilless mixes. They are generally based on peat moss or compost, with varying amounts of perlite, vermiculite, or pine bark mixed in. These sterile mixes are very moisture-retentive. Being lighter in weight (although they become heavier when wet), they make it easier to move smaller pots or hanging baskets. These lightweight mixes also make sense for a rooftop or balcony situation, or even for vertical wall containers hung on fences, where weight is a consideration. Such mixes are fairly expensive, so it's not economical to use them in large containers or raised beds. And because of their sterile nature, they quickly run out of the essential nutrients plants need, which are normally found in adequate amounts in mineral topsoils.

By either amending ground-level beds, creating your own custom soil mixes, or using lightweight, soilless mixes you will have an excellent garden easily worked by anyone. This is the most important step, and it is hard work perhaps better hired out to the kid down the block who's on the high school wrestling team. However it's done, do not cut corners on this step. With good soil the plants will pretty much care for themselves, and your garden experiences will be all the good things we know it can be.

*T*he Plants

Now that you have great soil, you can delve into the wonderful variety of plants and make the difficult choices about what to grow—difficult because there's always something else to try. Yes, I, too, suffer from catalog fever. My eyes are always bigger than my pocketbook and my yard. Worse yet, I work at a public garden, where I am constantly tempted by the newest variety and the plant collected from a faraway land. It's a rough job!

In the following sections, each of the major garden plant groups is briefly discussed, with an eye toward particular favorites and how they and others relate to the Enabling Garden. There are at least a dozen excellent books on each of the following groups of plants, as well as specialty books on single genuses. For example, within the broad area of perennial gardening, you can find entire reference works on daylilies alone, or on irises or hostas. There are enthusiasts for just about any plant. You will need to seek out these references as your interests evolve. You also need to know what is best grown and how in your part of the country. All of my practical gardening has taken place in the Chicago area, so the following will naturally be somewhat biased. Also, I don't want to take all the challenge and guesswork out of selecting plants for your own garden. Try the different; stretch the limits of what can be grown in your area. Learn from failures as well as successes. This, too, is what gardening is all about.

Vegetables

Perhaps the most rewarding and therapeutic group of plants to grow are vegetables. Rewarding, because they enable us to literally create life in the planting of the seed, follow the daily growth and changes as the plant quickly matures, and finally reap a tangible harvest we can eat and share with others. Therapeutic, because they keep us active in their day-to-day care, then offer us nutrition in the fresh fruits and vegetables we harvest. We do eat better when we grow our own food because we tend to eat what we grow. Children eat even spinach they've grown themselves. The real miracle to me is that it all happens so quickly: Most vegetables are considered annuals because they complete their entire life cycles in one growing season.

In your Enabling Garden, you can grow most any vegetable, depending on your climate and, quite literally, your taste: Grow what you want to eat. Vegetables do take considerable work, compared with other types of plants, so locate them in the most accessible areas of your garden. For me, these would be my larger raised beds and other containers. Even smaller containers work just fine. You can grow five radishes in a six-inch pot in less than a month, and ten lettuce plants in a half-barrel in less than 2 months.

For the more mobile and active gardener, simply grow taller varieties of vegetables or use supports for vining crops like cucumbers to bring them within reach for harvest without stooping. As I said before, avoid growing taller varieties of plants such as tomatoes in raised beds or other containers when the harvest may be out of your reach. Where space and energy is limited, concentrate on the most productive vegetables, such as squash, tomatoes, and green beans, as opposed to eggplants and green peppers, where harvests are usually smaller. I grow my tomatoes in ground-level beds. My wife helps with initial planting, but thereafter, I can reach them for care and harvest. I grow pole beans rather than bush beans the same way and for the same reasons, although with my PVC-pipe seed planter, I am able to plant larger seeds myself. If you can't afford larger raised beds and other planters, the above techniques bring a great many vegetables within reach.

Many varieties of vegetables are bred to be smaller in size and, therefore, perhaps more suitable for containers. Such varieties are less productive because of their smaller size. Furthermore, with large enough containers and raised beds, normal sized varieties do just fine. Although the nonvining, or bush types, of beans, squash, or cucumbers, for example, are best to grow. You can grow a full-size tomato plant in a 3-gallon plastic pail. This is one reason I stressed buying or making the largest raised beds or other containers you could afford. It makes the economics of production better—not great, but better—and doesn't restrict what you grow as much as smaller containers do.

Consider perennial vegetable varieties to lessen long-term effort. I plan next year to make a 4 x 8-foot bed raised 12 inches high with planks, digging down an additional 12 inches and mixing this soil with compost and manure, to contain my favorite spring vegetable, asparagus! I figure it will be raised high enough for me to easily harvest the wonderful, tender, fresh, green spears with my long-handled cut-and-hold pruners, but not so high as to interfere with hardiness. A good asparagus bed should last ten years, so it's worth the initial investment.

This technique should work just as well with any other deep-rooted, perennial vegetable. This simple raised bed would also be effective for many other types of gardening. In fact, I think the next one I do will be for strawberries. The extra 12 inches of digging won't be necessary, just some loosening of my heavy clay soil, and then I'll have my favorite fresh spring fruit, too.

My favorite crops are what we call cold crops, performing best in cool weather and withstanding several frosts. They enable us here in Chicago to extend our growing season in the spring and fall. Included are the following:

- Bibb or semiheading lettuce
- Broccoli
- Cabbage
- Collards
- Head lettuce
- Leeks
- Peas
- Shallots
- Bok choy
- Brussels sprouts
- Carrots
- Garlic
- Leaf lettuce
- Onions
- Radishes
- Spinach

These crops can be planted from seed or transplanted as soon as you can work the soil in the spring. I have planted as early as April 1, particularly in raised beds and other containers that warm up more quickly than ground-level beds in the spring. You can replant many of these crops in mid- to late summer for fall harvests that mature as the weather cools. One of my very favorite long-season vegetables is leeks, which I plant from seed as early in April as possible and harvest just before the ground freezes in the fall.

During the summer my time goes, first and foremost, into raising tomatoes. I have a couple of favorite varieties I grow every year, but I also select a new one to try and top the flavor of the old standby. Ripe tomatoes, being brightly colored, are easily distinguished from green foliage. Many varieties grow tall enough, when supported, to be managed at a height within most people's reach.

A couple of seed companies specializing in tomato seeds will tempt and challenge you with over 1,500 known varieties. There are sizes and shapes and colors of all kinds, so no garden need be without them. Ask a bunch of vegetable gardeners what they look forward to most, and the majority say to bite into the first truly ripe, warm-from-the-vine tomato of the summer. I like many other warm-season vegetables, but I *must* have my tomatoes.

Tomatoes love warm soil, so we in the Enabling Garden can do a better job of growing them. Our containers and raised beds stay warmer than ground-level beds because they are exposed to warmer air, and sunlight heats up their sides. This creates warmer soil, on which tomatoes and other warm-season crops thrive.

Beyond the preceding basic suggestions, it is very difficult to recommend a list of vegetables because of your individual likes and dislikes and better local performers, so I won't. *Do* use varieties that are the most productive given limited space, resist local insects and diseases, and are best suited to your growing season and conditions.

Vegetables that are brightly colored when ripe, such as golden zucchini squash, red leaf lettuce, and purple-podded beans, stand out from the surrounding green foliage for the visually impaired gardener. Amazingly enough to a sighted person, several blind gardeners I worked with were able to tell ripe tomatoes at a distance by smell alone!

Depending upon the time and energy available, vegetable gardening can provide most of your fresh, frozen, and canned needs year-round. On the other hand, it can merely consist of a small plot that gives you a few fresh salads or, at minimum, a single tomato plant in a bucket that gives you several pounds of nature's finest. *Everyone* should experience raising their own food. With comfortable soil heights and selected tools and techniques, the Enabling Garden permits everyone to have this opportunity.

The best advice is to start small and grow only what you want to eat fresh and share with others. Perhaps later you will grow enough to preserve, which is an entirely different, rewarding activity in itself.

Bulbs

Bulbs, with related corms and tubers, are one of my favorite groups of plants for the Enabling Garden because beyond planting them properly, there is little else to do but sit back and enjoy them. Some are the first messengers of spring and, if carefully selected, can provide many weeks of bloom when little else is happening in the garden. Many are fragrant and make excellent cut flowers, as well. For the purposes of our discussion, I will stick to those bulbs that are cold-hardy perennials, rather than those that in cold climates must be dug in the fall and stored where they won't freeze, like dahlias, cannas, or tuberoses. These are indeed fine plants, but I barely have time to get the rest of my garden ready for winter, without digging and storing bulbs, too.

I use bulbs to extend my spring growing season. Most commonly, bulbs are used for very early spring color, as given by narcissus, tulips, and crocuses. After a long, cold, dark winter, the thrill of brightly colored spring bulbs is a very important uplift.

I generally prefer bulbs that reliably come back year after year, as well as those that also reseed or multiply readily. I avoid those that are favorite snack foods of the rabbits and deer that live in our neighborhood. I have tried various animal repellants, but, besides the expense, the deer seem to get used to them, so why bother buying and spraying the stuff in the first place? I just avoid using the plants they eat; like crocuses, tulips, and dog-tooth violets (*Erythronium*), but I have many other choices the deer seem to avoid.

Various types of bulbs tend to do better in cooler areas, where they get deep enough winter cold for proper development. Check local information on bulbs that do best in your area. Also, bear in mind that some otherwise hardy bulbs will not survive aboveground in small or large containers through very cold winters where the container soil freezes solid. Plant a few in various types of containers to experiment; identify those that do best for you. The larger the container and the milder the climate, the better the chances. Because of the work involved in planting, I don't like to have the things die, so I do all of my bulb gardening in my ground-level beds. I plant most myself, but because it's a onetime investment, I seek help planting bulbs in out-of-reach places.

The far southern states have different bulb choices because warmer climates don't provide the cold period needed by many northern bulbs to flower. Southern gardeners must refrigerate such bulbs in pots, much as I do to force bulbs indoors. However, in the South you can grow many tropical bulbs outdoors that I must confine to the greenhouse. My mother-in-law grew several kinds of amaryllis in backyard beds in Baton Rouge, Louisiana. I guess it all tends to balance out.

Lilies are an important group of flowering bulbs. Many are very fragrant. By careful variety and type selection, you can have flowers in a rainbow of colors from late spring through midfall, on plants ranging from 18 inches to well over 6 feet. They can be grown in most parts of the country and are very effective garden plants.

Many bulbs are somewhat toxic, mostly in the bulb itself or its onion-skinlike paper covering, as opposed to the shoots and flowers. This helps them avoid being eaten by burrowing rodents, so care should be taken when handling bulbs with sensitive skin and where small children might eat them. Once planted, I wouldn't worry about it.

The only other disadvantage to growing many spring bulbs, including narcissus and tulips, is their ephemeral nature. Properly grown, they sprout flowers, set seed, and generally go dormant during the hotter, drier times of the summer. Unsightly foliage hangs on and gradually dies as the bulbs go dormant, leaving open spaces in the garden when the process is complete. This foliage must be left on, however, to regenerate the bulb for the following year's leaves and flowers. The unsightliness of dying bulb foliage can be avoided in two ways. One is to plant minor, or small, bulbs, such as crocus, scillas, and dwarf varieties of tulips and narcissus. By their naturally smaller size, they seem to go dormant more quickly, while their aboveground parts seem to just dry up and disappear. The very early bloomers, like snowdrops, snow crocus, and *Puschkinia*, also seem to go dormant very quickly. The other way to avoid the foliage problem is to plant your bulbs near and around other plants—such as hostas, ferns, and other perennials, as well as annuals (or vise versa)—whose later emerging foliage and flowers ultimately hide the bulb foliage and the subsequent empty spaces in beds and borders. This way you can easily get two seasons of color out of the same space—especially important in a small garden.

When considering the kinds of bulbs and where to plant them in your Enabling Garden, bear the following in mind.

1. Who's going to plant them? It's hard work. I plant mostly minor bulbs, like snowdrops, scillas, crocuses, chionodoxas, or puschkinias, which require digging only to 3 to 5 inches deep. I plant fewer narcissus, which require 8 to digging 10 inches deep. That's a big difference when planting a clump of ten or more, where you dig a single large hole. In any case, much deeper than this, and I can't reach to place the bulb in the hole right-side up. Therefore, I usually plant bulbs with my wife or a friend, who, as I dig or predig holes, follows along and places the bulbs properly. Then I cover them over.

   A couple of tools are specially made for bulb planting. An electric drill (cordless is easiest) can take a large auger, 2 to 3 inches in diameter and about 18 inches long. This enables you to drill a hole to the correct depth in the soil; then just place the bulb in and cover it. The hole tends to collapse in well-amended soil, so I find this tool more useful for shallow planting. The other bulb tool is a long-handled bulb planter, discussed in the tool chapter, useful for digging bulb holes up to 6 inches deep. I find it difficult to plant narcissus and tulips because they must be 8 to 10 inches deep in our area. The tool isn't long enough, and in amended soil, again, the deeper hole tends to collapse.

2. Plant in random, natural clumps rather than straight rows. Also make odd- rather than even-numbered clumps. Nature rarely works in straight rows or even numbers. However, you may desire the formal effect of rows as is often done with tulips and hyacinths.

3. If you are limited to a few locations, try to site spring-blooming bulbs where they will be visible from indoors or places you frequent while outdoors. This is particularly helpful with smaller bulbs like snowdrops, snow crocuses, and winter aconites, which tend to get lost when viewed from afar.

4. If possible, select fragrant varieties of bulbs. Use them as cut flowers, or locate them near paths or porches, where the scent will be brought to your nose with the slightest breeze. Brightly colored and more fragrant varieties are appreciated by people who are visually impaired or blind.

5. Select varieties that collectively can provide a lengthy season of spring bloom. For example, growing the narcissus varieties 'February Gold,' followed by 'Mount Hood,' followed by 'Actea,' then finally late-flowering 'Geranium' or 'Baby Moon' results in almost two months of narcissus. You can also stretch the season to three months by growing bulbs that bloom in sequence, such as this series: snowdrops, aconite, scilla, chionodoxa, puschkinia, narcissus, and frittilaria. Of course, various combinations of types and colors are also effective.

You can plan on chionodoxa and 'Dutch Master' narcissus blooming reliably at the same time. That's where your design creativity comes in.

6. Culturally, most bulbs require excellent drainage. Bulbs are best suited for garden areas that are on the dry side during summer. They also need full sun during the time they are in bloom. Early bulbs planted under trees complete most of their cycle before the trees leaf out and become shady.

7. Hybrid tulips and hyacinths are very effective for one or two years, then gradually decline. Fewer will come up each year, and fewer still will flower. This is because they have been bred to produce extra-large blooms, which greatly deplete the bulb's energy. The foliage does not have enough time to fully regenerate the bulb. Hence, the flowers decrease in size over the course of several years, and the plant may not flower at all.

Following are some of my favorite bulbs and some characteristics:

Allium (onion family) This too-little-used group of bulbs provides low-maintenance, perennial color from late spring through the fall. They come in a wide range of colors and sizes, from the 6- to 8-inch *Allium moly* to the over-3-foot *Allium giganteum*. They generally prefer full sun and drier soils. Their flower heads bloom up to two weeks and are composed of many tiny, individual florets. Some allium flowers are fragrant; all the bulbs, leaves, and stems in this group smell like onions when bruised. *Alliums* worth a try include these:

Allium species	Color	Bloom time	Height (inches)
A. *aflatunense*	lilac purple	April-May	20–30
A. *caeruleum*	deep blue	May-June	20
A. *giganteum*	purple	May-June	40
A. *moly*	bright yellow	May-June	10
A. *neapolitanum*	white	April-June	15
A. *ostrowskianum*	rose pink	May-June	8
A. *sphaerocephalon*	red-purple	June-July	20
A. *thunbergii*	'Ozawa' pink	Sept-Nov	12

Anemone (windflower) These flowers are white, blue, or pink, daisy-like, and 1½ inches across. The plants grow 4 inches tall and flower in April. Anemones are best planted under trees and shrubs in masses. They tend to slowly spread, but not invasively.

Chionodoxa (glory-of-the-snow) As the common name indicates, this wonderful bulb flowers very early in the spring (March-April), often through late snows. The ¾-inch flowers are light or dark blue with white centers. Each stem has 8 to 15 flowers. The overall plant is 5 to 8 inches tall and is best planted in groups under trees and shrubs and in borders. They are easily hidden by other plants as they go dormant. One of my favorites.

Crocus This is among the most popular spring bulbs, although some species flower in the fall. The diminutive, 3- to 5-inch plants bloom March-April and come in a range of colors, including yellow, white, purple striped, and bronze. They can be planted almost anywhere in well-drained soil, including the lawn, where they will naturalize. Care must be taken to let their foliage die down before cutting the lawn, so next year's flowers are provided energy. The two most common species are snow crocus (*crysanthus*), the earliest to bloom, and Dutch crocus (*vernus*), which follows two to three weeks later. Some of the better varieties include: 'Snowbunting' (white), 'Skyline' (deep blue with white stripes), and the Dutch crocuses: 'Joan of Arc' (white), 'Remembrance' (blue-violet), 'Pickwick' (pale blue with white stripes), 'Purpureus' (violet purple).

Eranthus (winter aconite) These tiny 2- to 3-inch, yellow-flowered plants bloom in March, often appearing through the snow. They bloom at the same time as snowdrops. They are favored because of their very early yellow color.

Erythronium (dog's-tooth violet, trout lily) The plants grow 8 to 10 inches, usually with one pair of leaves emerging at the base. The leaves are often mottled, providing interest even when not in bloom. The common wildflower varieties have been hybridized into good garden plants, including 'White Beauty' (white), 'Pagoda' (golden yellow), 'Purple King' (purple with white center), and 'Lilac Wonder'.

Galanthus (snowdrop) One of my favorite bulbs because it is the very first to bloom here in Chicago, often as early as the beginning of February if planted in a warm spot and we have a mild winter. They have tiny, pendulous, white flowers carried on 4-inch stems. Plant snowdrops in clumps of ten or more to be visible; otherwise, they tend to get lost.

Hyacinth (Dutch hyacinth) One of the most popular spring bulbs. The overall plant height is about 12 inches, including a 6- to 8-inch flower spike composed of many individual, 3/4-inch florets. Hyacinths bloom in April in Chicago and come in a range of colors, from bright blue, violet, and white to pink, red, yellow, and orange. Their chief attribute in the garden is their intense, sweet fragrance. A few clumps of 5 or 6 bulbs in strategic places can fill your garden with heady fragrance. Hyacinths are often forced for bloom indoors as well.

Iris This genus includes a relatively small group of brightly colored, early spring bulbs. One primary species, *Iris danfordiae*, is bright yellow. The other is *Iris reticulata*, the best varieties of which include 'Harmony' (blue), 'Cantab' (light blue), and 'Joyce' (deep violet blue). Each bulb produces two or three flowers on 5-inch stems. The narrow, straplike foliage remaining after bloom is easily hidden among other plants. Their bright early-season colors are more easily seen by the visually impaired. Bulbous irises are best planted in clumps of ten or more because of their small size.

Lilium (lilies) This is an exciting group of summer-fall blooming bulbs, brightly colored and many with wonderful scents. The one most familiar to us is the Easter lily. By carefully selecting varieties, you can have lilies in flower most of the growing season. The taller ones place themselves within easier reach of the eye and nose. Plant lilies in groups of 3 to 7 for best effect in the garden. Rabbits and deer love them as much as people, so they are best avoided where the little beasties will eat them and cause disappointment and frustration we don't need. A few of the best varieties include these:

Variety or species	Color	Bloom time	Height (feet)
'Black Dragon'	white and maroon	July	6–8
candidum	white (fragrant)	June	3–4
'Casablanca'	white (very fragrant)	August	4–6
'Citronella'	lemon yellow	July	4–5
'Classic'	lemon yellow	late June	4–5
'Corsica'	pink (fragrant)	June	2
'Elf'	pink	June	2–3
'Golden Splendor'	gold (very fragrant)	July	4–5
'Journey's End'	crimson pink	August	4–5
'Red Duchess'	red	June	3–4
'Star Gazer'	crimson (fragrant)	July	2–3
'White Henryi'	white (fragrant)	July–August	4–5

Narcissus (daffodils, jonquils) Popular and commonly used, there are literally hundreds of varieties of varying hardiness that can be grown in many areas of the country. Overall plant height, flowering time, and color depend on the variety grown, with yellow, white, red, orange, and pink being the dominant colors. Narcissuses require well-drained soil, in full sun to partial shade, and they prefer to be kept dry when dormant. Selected varieties can provide flowers throughout the March-May flowering period. Depending upon the variety, plants have 1 to 8 flowers per stem. Their main advantages in the Enabling Garden are their bright, easily seen colors, long life, fragrance in some varieties, and low maintenance. Once planted, they will provide many years of enjoyment with little care. They are longlasting cut flowers that brighten up the indoors, too. If I had the choice of only one type of bulb to plant in my garden, I would choose narcissus. The following are some of the best varieties:

'Baby Moon'	golden yellow (fragrant)
'Carlton'	yellow with gold cup
'Cheerfulness'	white (fragrant)
'Dutch Master'	golden yellow
'February Gold'	golden yellow (early)
'February Silver'	white with yellow cup
'Geranium'	white with orange cup (fragrant)
'Ice Follies'	white with yellow cup
'King Alfred'	yellow
'Liberty Bells'	lemon yellow
'Minnow'	lemon yellow (fragrant)
'Mount Hood'	ivory white
'Salome'	white with salmon cup
'Thalia'	white (fragrant)
'Trevithian'	lemon yellow (fragrant)

Puschkinia This small, minor bulb blooms March-April. Bluish-white flowers cluster on 4-inch stems. They tolerate partial shade so are excellent under trees and shrubs. They also reseed in fertile soil, but not invasively.

Scilla (squill) This native Siberian is known for its very intense blue flowers during March and April. Left undisturbed, the plants reseed themselves, over time forming large masses of unsurpassed early spring color. They tolerate shade and combine well with other spring bulbs.

Tulipa (tulip) Tulips are the most popular bulbs worldwide. There are thousands of varieties to choose from, ranging in height from 5 to 24 inches. They are useful as cut flowers in a wide spectrum of colors—yellow, red, pink, white, and lavender, with many containing a mixture of colors. Most large-flowered hybrid tulips tend to fade away over the years because the bulb puts so much energy into flower production that it does not have the time to fully renew itself before dormancy sets in. This requires a new investment in replacement bulbs and repeat digging and planting at 8 to 10 inches. They are a favorite snack food of deer, so they are a challenge to grow if deer are around. I cannot grow tulips in my yard because of the deer. Nonetheless, this group because of its range of colors and types and its ease of culture, offers something for almost everyone. Some of the best varieties include these:

'Apeldoorn'	brilliant red
'Apricot Beauty'	salmon pink
'Bellona'	yellow (fragrant)
'Black Parrot'	violet black
'Cordell Hull'	red and white
'General DeWitt'	orange (fragrant)
'Heart's Delight'	red and white
'Jacqueline'	pink
'Jeantine'	red and apricot
'Jimmy'	luminous orange
'Peerless Pink'	pink
'Prins Carnaval'	yellow with red flame
'Red Emperor'	red
'Red Riding Hood'	deep red
'Red Sprite'	red
'Spring Green'	green and white
'Temple of Beauty'	salmon orange
'Texas Gold'	bright yellow
'West Point'	yellow

Bulbs are a marvelous group of plants that engage you with their bright spring and summer colors and sweet fragrances. Their easy culture and low-maintenance characteristics make them ideal for your Enabling Garden. If you can't plant them yourself, it's worth it to have someone help you because early bulbs officially end the winter.

Annuals

The most common group of plants found in gardens are annuals. An extremely diverse group, including such favorites as marigolds and zinnias, annuals are classified as flowering plants that complete their life cycle in one year (seed, to plant, to flower, to seed), then die. Included in this group are tropical and perennial plants that would grow continually in their native locations but are killed by fall frosts in cold areas. The common impatiens is one of these.

In your Enabling Garden, the best annuals are those that flower over the longest season possible to maximize color and prevent empty space. This is particularly important in small containers, where perhaps only a few plants can be used, and even larger containers, where season-long color is desired. Annuals are also the best choice for seasonal color in containers and raised beds in very cold winter areas, where many permanent plants would be killed as the containers freeze solid.

Annuals are available in a total range of colors, sizes, textures, forms, and fragrances. I enjoy poring over seed catalogs to mix and match annual combinations for my containers and ground-level beds seeking just the right combinations of color, fragrance, bloom time, and forms. There are annuals for virtually any garden site, including moist, dry, shady, and sunny ones, and any combination thereof. Finally, when the right plants are in the right places and are given the care they need, they are easy to grow.

While you can grow many annuals from seed, transplants are readily available and inexpensive at most garden centers. A flat of transplants can go a long way in your garden if you select varieties that ultimately grow larger to cover more space. Most garden centers allow you to mix and match, enabling you to pick just the right combinations in the exact numbers you need. A common marketing ploy used by sellers of annuals is to have them in flower in the flats by sale time. This lets the customer know the flower colors, but it often causes the plant stress, which may delay further growth and flowering. I prefer knowing by name what I am looking for and seeking out younger plants before they flower. At the very least, the first flowers at sale time are usually best pinched off at planting to encourage branching and new blooms.

The only disadvantage to annuals is that they require replacing each year, which is an added expense and perhaps an unwanted chore. Most of my annuals are in containers, with only a few here and there in ground-level beds to add color. For example, under a large, flowering crabapple tree in my front yard, I have a shade garden that tends to be somewhat drab in mid- and late summer. I have left pockets where I plant a few shade-loving annuals. My low-maintenance favorite is impatiens. Once planted, they are soon covered with hundreds of self- shedding blooms, each plant covering considerable space until frost takes them in the fall.

This brings up another important consideration when selecting annuals for your Enabling Garden. Annuals and many other plants benefit from routine removal of dead blossoms and pinching back to encourage branching and new flowers. Many annual dianthus plants are literally covered with blossoms early in the summer. If they are not removed when faded, the plant sets seed and, with its life cycle complete, stops flowering, declines, and dies leaving gaps in your planting. Removing the blossoms fools the plant into trying to set more seed, so it produces more blossoms. Coleus is a useful garden annual whose multicolored foliage is its most effective part. As the growing season progresses, the plant sets flowers at the top of each branch. These are best removed to encourage branching and more of the desirable foliage.

The message here is that if you have the time to do these chores, great. They are useful activities that keep you engaged in your garden. In a smaller patio or balcony garden, you may deliberately select plants that provide this activity, in order to exercise your hands and hand-eye coordination. Fifteen minutes or so every few days may be all that's needed for this routine grooming. Other gardeners may choose those annuals that, beyond planting and water needs, care for themselves. Many varieties of hybrid plants are sterile, or do not set seed, which forces the plants to continue trying (continue flowering) with or without dead blooms removed. Still others, such as the large spiderflower (*Cleome*), keep flowering the entire season in spite of being covered with seedpods.

Another group of annuals you should be aware of are those that perform best in cooler weather, such as pansies, flowering kale, and pot marigolds. This is an advantage because you can set out the plants when there is still risk of a few frosts. These early-flowering annuals are an excellent way to bring color to your garden long before the summer annuals and other plants take over. You can create envious combinations with early annuals and spring bulbs. This cold-adapted characteristic is also their downfall because as warmer weather sets in, these plants gradually decline, requiring replacement. Some newer varieties of pansies (one of my favorite spring flowers), though, if planted where they get some shade in the afternoon, will hang in there most of the summer in cooler areas, particularly if you remove spent blooms.

The following lists of annuals are by no means complete. Again, entire books and videos are available on the subject. The ones listed have some particularly outstanding sensory characteristics and are organized by light requirements. Those marked "high-maintenance" benefit from having spent blossoms removed or being pinched back regularly.

Some of my favorite combinations are: red salvia, white periwinkle, and blue lobelia; yellow begonias and blue lobelia; blue or red salvia with yellow marigolds; Mexican sunflower, dusty miller, and blue salvia; burning bush, heliotrope, and white dianthus; blue salvia and pink flowering tobacco; and pink geraniums and dusty miller.

There are many great annuals, and the preceding is only a short listing. Many are good for cut flowers, pressing, or drying. There are some suitable for every purpose in your garden. Annuals are particularly suitable for containers because of their generally shallow root systems. Consult the many displays I'm sure you will find in your neighborhood for ideas. The many hundreds of seed catalogs you can get for free will also be great sources of suggestions. They begin to arrive in January and can help lessen the winter blahs as you dream of the spring to come.

*A*nnuals

Name	Scent	Texture	Color	High-Maintenance
FULL SUN				
Amaranth		●	●	·
Burning bush		●		
Cleome		●	●	
Cockscomb		●	●	
Cosmos		●	●	●
Dianthus	●		●	●
Dusty miller		●	●	
Flowering kale		●	●	
Flowering tobacco	●		●	●
Geranium	●		●	
Globe amaranth		●	●	
Heliotrope	●		●	
Marigold	●		●	●
Mexican sunflower			●	
Mignonette	●			
Moss rose			●	
Petunia			●	●
Pot marigold			●	
Sanvitalia			●	
Snapdragon	●		●	●
Strawflower		●	●	●
Sweet alyssum	●		●	
Zinnia			●	●
SUN TO PARTIAL SHADE				
Ageratum		●	●	
Begonia			●	
Four-o'clock	●		●	
Lobelia			●	
Pansy	●		●	●
Periwinkle			●	
Salvia		●	●	●
PARTIAL SHADE TO SHADE				
Begonia			●	
Browallia			●	
Coleus		●	●	●
Impatiens			●	
Monkey flower			●	

Perennials

If backed into a corner and asked to choose one group of plants and no other to have in my garden, I would probably select perennials. Perennials, if properly chosen to match your climate, reliably come back year to year despite being killed to the ground during the winter. They are my favorites for the following reasons.

- By virtue of its indefinite lifespan, a perennial is a one-time investment. Of course, some are longer-lived than others, and if a particular favorite succumbs for some reason, I will replace it.

- Perennials gradually increase in size over the years, allowing one of the most enjoyable and rewarding aspects of gardening, namely, sharing with friends. Exchanging plant divisions not only extends your enthusiasm for a plant to someone else, but introduces you to new plants and, potentially, new people. Notice I said perennials *gradually* increase in size. Given the chance, some perennials will eat up your garden in no time at all. Innocent plants in heavy, poor soils in one part of the country may be terribly invasive planted in richer soils in another region. Some are prohibited by law because not even the native plants can compete with them if they escape your garden. Purple loosestrife is a local noxious weed often grown in gardens; since escaping, it is now choking out our wetlands. Avoid invasive plants in your Enabling Garden because they will be too much work to keep in check. Be careful at plant giveaways and exchanges so you don't accept things eating up someone else's garden.

- There are perennials for nearly every garden environment and style. Both in flower and leaf, every color of the rainbow is represented, from the softest pastels to the brightest, boldest shades, accommodating every visual ability and personal taste. You can find low-lying, creeping perennials a couple of inches tall and monsters over 10 feet. Some are strongly vertical in shape, others are round, and still more are a combination of the two. Textures range from the soft and feathery to the extremes of bold and coarse, stimulating your senses of sight and touch.

- Some perennials bloom with the melting of the spring snows, like *Adonis*, others, like *Tricyrtis*, bloom well into fall. Some can be counted on for several months of bloom on their own, and most others for at least a couple of weeks. There is a long list of excellent cut flowers among perennials.

- Many perennials offer delights for the nose, from the delicately scented peony to the heavy lily. Some release their fragrance with the first rays of the morning sun, while others will tempt you at night.

- Some perennials have excellent fall color, such as the bright yellow *Amsonia* foliage. Others like *Sedum* 'Autumn Joy' and various *Rudbeckias*, remain standing during the winter, offering dried seed and flower heads, giving you an additional effective season in your garden.

- On the degree-of-work scale, perennials require less than vegetables and annuals but more than trees and shrubs. There is no such thing as a no-maintenance garden, but once planted, perennials do permit you a certain amount of sitting back and enjoying. Removing dead blossoms regularly makes them look better (unless you're anticipating decorative seedheads) and encourages longer blooming periods for some. Peonies can remain undisturbed for many years; my neighbor has plantings along his driveway that have been there over 100 years. You can often spot the location of a long-since-demolished farmhouse by still-visible iris, peony, and daylily plantings, which used to surround the house and delight the eye of a long-ago gardener.

Hardy asters, on the other hand, must be divided every couple of years or so. Many perennials need this chore every three to five years depending on soil type, climate, and vigor of the plant itself. I usually divide my perennials right in the ground, cutting pieces off the main clump with a freshly sharpened spade, while leaving what remains undisturbed. I refill the holes with compost, which enriches the soil around the plants. This division process saves a great deal of effort.

❁ Perennials mix well with every other group of plants, making them extremely versatile in your Enabling Garden or any other landscape. In a bed of annuals, perennials can offer an interesting color or textural contrast. In the shrub border, they add color during the times when the shrubs lack bloom, and/or create effective combinations of forms or textures. Perennials planted adjacent to bulbs will hide declining bulb foliage and take over empty spots.

It is this near-infinite variety, of opportunities and types, with new perennials being introduced each year, that provides a great deal of intellectual challenge. Seeking the unusual and rare, and designing the perennial border with the perfect balance of color, form, and texture through every day of the growing season, exercises our creativity and knowledge. Combine perennials with basic color harmonies and blooming times that coincide. Design complementary contrasts in color, form, and texture in foliage, alone as a specimen, or in combination with other plants. Such challenges provide me with many hours of enjoyment. Not only are perennials popular with me, but if there's a garden subject with more written about it than perennials, let me know. Perennials alone can offer a lifetime of gardening challenges and enjoyment.

When I selected mine, I looked for several specific qualities.

❁ Long blooming season to enhance effectiveness in the garden, like perennial geraniums or *Dicentra* 'Luxuriant'.

❁ If the space is available, choose larger, bold perennials—such as perennial sunflowers, hollyhocks, larger ornamental grasses, and joe-pye-weed—for effect from a distance or to stand tall behind shorter companions. Larger plants contribute grand scale and drama to beds and borders, and even standing alone as specimens in the lawn.

❁ Plants requiring higher maintenance are fine as long as I can reach them. Choose low-maintenance plants like Siberian iris or false indigo for garden areas more difficult to reach.

*F*avorite Perennials

The following are listed by genus, with common names following. Each genus may have many species, varieties, and cultivars of varying quality, flower color, and overall form. Check detailed references to make final selections.

Name	Color	Height	Bloom time	Scent Y/N	Light	Comments
Achillea, yarrow	golden/yellow	2–3′	summer	N	sun	Tough plant, good cut flowers, dries well. 'Coronation Gold' and 'Moonshine' are good cultivars.
Aconitum, monkshood	blue	3–5′	late summer into fall	N	shade–partial sun	All parts poisonous, great late blue color. *Arendsii, carmichaelii,* and *napellus* don't need staking.
Adenophera, lady bells	blue	1–3′	summer	Y	sun–partial shade	Very long-lived, and long-flowering season.
Adonis, pheasant's eye	yellow	12″	early spring	N	sun–partial shade	One of the earliest perennials to bloom, poisonous.
Ajuga, bugleweed	blue	4–12″	late spring	N	sun–shade	Good ground cover, many good varieties. 'Burgundy Glow' has cream, pink, and burgundy leaves.
Alcea, hollyhock	various	5–10′	summer into fall	N	sun	Great old-fashioned plant for back of the border, reseeds (actually a biennial).
Alchemilla, lady's mantle	yellow	1–2′	early spring	N	sun–partial shade	Outstanding foliage texture, holds rain-drops, reseeds. Use as accent to stronger colors.
Amsonia	blue	3′	early summer	N	sun–partial shade	Great low-maintenance plant, yellow fall color.
Anemone, Japanese Anemone	white/pink	2–5′	late summer into fall	N	sun–partial shade	Try 'Honorine Jobert' or 'September Charm.' Good cut flower, low-maintenance, late-season color. Excellent with *Aconitum.*
Anemone, pasqueflower	purple	12″	early spring	N	sun–partial shade	Early bloomer, great fuzzy texture, feathery seedheads.
Anthemis, golden marguerite	yellow/white	1–3′	late spring into early fall	N	sun	Great long-season bloomer, cut flowers. 'Kelwayii' and 'E.C. Buxton' are good performers.
Aquilegia, columbine	various	1–4′	spring to early summer	N	sun–partial shade	Short-lived, readily reseeds, easy to grow. 'Hensoll Harebell', 'Yellow Queen', and 'Crystal' are reliable.

Plant	Color	Height	Bloom	Light	Fragrant	Comments
Arabis, rock cress	white	6–10"	spring	sun	Y	Front of the border, fragrant plant.
Arisaema, Jack-in-the-pulpit	purple	18"	spring	partial shade–shade	N	Unusual bloom, dependable wildflower, reseeds.
Artemisia, wormwood	silver foliage	1–4'	not applicable	sun	Y	Great texture, silver color blends well with others, cuts and dries well. Some are invasive.
Aruncus, goatsbeard	white	4–7'	early summer	sun–partial shade	N	Low-maintenance, large plant, soft texture.
Asclepias, milkweed	pink, red, orange	2–5'	summer into fall	sun	N	Tough plants, attractive to butterflies.
Aster	white, purple, blue, pink	6"–6'	summer into fall	sun–partial shade	N	Great late-summer color, many kinds available. 'Monch,' 'Hella Lacy,' 'Professor Kippenburg,' and 'Alma Potsche' usually do not need staking.
Astilbe	white, pink, red	6"–5'	summer	sun–partial shade	N	Great soft-textured, feathery blooms.
Baptisia, false indigo	blue, white	3–6'	early summer	sun	N	Low-maintenance plant, interesting seedpods, cut flowers.
Bergenia	pink	18"	spring	sun–shade	N	Cabbage-like leaves, bold texture.
Boltonia, false aster	pale pink	3–5'	late summer into fall	sun	N	Covered with flowers during late season. I like 'Cattleya,' 'Pumila,' and 'Peach Blossom.'
Campanula, bellflower	blue, white	6"–4'	spring and summer	sun–partial shade	N	Many kinds available, one of the better sources of blue in the garden. 'Blue Chips' is a nice edger or cascading plant.
Cassia, senna	yellow	6'	summer	sun–partial shade	N	Bees love it. Large, shrublike, low-maintenance, interesting compound foliage. Seedpods effective in winter.
Centranthus, red valerian	red, white	2–3'	late spring to early fall	sun–partial shade	Y	Long-blooming, fragrant.
Cephelaria	pale yellow	6–8'	midsummer	sun	N	Tall, undemanding, airy-textured plant for the back of the border.
Chelone, turtlehead	pink	2–4'	late summer to fall	partial shade	N	Unusual flower, low-maintenance, prefers moist soil.
Chrysanthemum, mum	various	1–3'	late summer to fall	sun	Y	Excellent for fall color and cut flowers. Some are fragrant.
Cimicifuga, snakeroot	white	2–8'	summer through fall	sun–shade	Y	Tall, stately, vertical effect. 'White Pearl' and 'Atropurpurea' are favorites.

Name	Color	Height	Bloom time	Scent Y/N	Light	Comments
Convallaria, lily-of-the-valley	white	8″	spring	Y	shade–partial shade	Very fragrant, poisonous, possibly invasive groundcover.
Coreopsis, tickseed	yellow	6″–3′	spring into fall	N	sun	Useful group, some invasive, very floriferous.
Delphinium	various	3–8′	spring and summer	N	sun	Avoid those needing staking. Generally short lived, can be magnificent.
Dianthus, sweet William	pink, white, red	1–2′	late spring into summer	Y	sun	Fragrant low edging plant, requires deadheading for best performance.
Dicentra, bleeding heart	pink, white	2–3′	spring through summer	N	sun–shade	Excellent low-maintenance plant, good combination with Brunnera, unusual flower, some long-blooming.
Digitalis, foxglove	yellow, pink	2–4′	summer	N	sun–partial shade	Strong vertical form, reseeds, poisonous. Ambigua and purpurea are popular.
Dodecatheon, shooting-star	pink, white	15″	late spring	N	partial shade–shade	Unusual nodding, dart-shaped flower.
Doronicum, leopard's-bane	yellow	1–2′	spring	N	partial shade	Good source of early bright color, cut flowers.
Echinacea, purple coneflower	pink, purple, white	3′	summer	N	sun	Great cut flowers, low-maintenance. Butterflies love it. Large seedheads in winter, if the finches don't eat them. 'Magnus' and 'Alba' are nice together.
Epimedium, barrenwort	various	8–12″	spring	N	shade	Long-lived shade plant, ground cover, unusual flower.
Eupatorium, Joe-Pye-weed	purple, blue, white	1–6′	summer to early fall	N	sun–partial shade	Very attractive to butterflies, good for late color. Back of the border plant, grows very large if kept moist.
Ferns (many types)	foliage	6″–4′	not applicable	N	sun to shade	Unsurpassed for soft textural effect, softens bolder forms and colors, good in cut flower arrangements.
Gallardia, blanket flower	red, yellow	8″–2′	early summer to fall	N	sun	Long bloom season, bright color. 'Goblin' and 'Baby Cole' don't need staking.

Plant	Color	Height	Bloom time	Fragrant	Light	Notes
Geranium, cranesbill	pink, purple	1–2'	late spring and summer	N	sun to partial shade	Durable long bloomers, good for middle to front of the border, some fragrant. 'Johnson's Blue,' 'Striatum,' and 'Wargrave Pink' are good.
Gypsophila, baby's-breath	white, pink	1–3'	summer	N	sun	Covered with tiny blooms, great for soft-texture effect.
Heliopsis, false sunflower	yellow	2–5'	summer to early fall	N	sun	Great cut flowers, drought-tolerant, tough plant, good late color. 'Summer Sun' is one of the best.
Hemerocallis, daylily	yellow, orange, lavender, red		spring into fall	Y	sun to partial shade	Excellent group of plants, durable, long-lived, low-maintenance, does well in containers, hundreds of varieties available. 'Stella de Oro,' 'Happy Returns,' and 'May May' are good long-season bloomers.
Hesperis, dame's rocket	purple	3'	summer	Y	sun–partial shade	Reseeds, fragrant.
Heuchera, coralbells	various	2'	summer	N	sun–partial shade	Cut flowers, soft texture, long-lived, low-maintenance. 'June Bride' has white flowers, 'Palace Purple' and 'Coral Cloud' have textured foliage.
Hibiscus, rose mallow	white/pink, red	3–8'	summer to fall	N	sun	Giant, 12-inch flowers, very showy.
Hosta, plantain lily	lavender white	1–3'	late summer to fall	Y	sun–shade	Excellent shade plants, very many kinds, good cut flowers, some fragrant. Leaves and flowers good in arrangements.
Iris	various	4"–4'	spring through summer	N	sun–partial shade	Excellent group of border plants. The *siberica*, *ensata*, and *crestata* species are the most trouble-free and widely grown.
Lavendula, lavender	blue purple/ soft pink	15"	summer	Y	sun	A must for the fragrant garden, dry well for many uses.
Liastris, blazing star	purple	2–5'	summer to fall	N	sun	Great cut flowers, attractive to butterflies, native prairie plant. 'Kobold' and 'Alba' are popular.
Ligularia	orange-yellow	3–6'	summer	Y	sun–partial shade	Moisture-loving, good cut flowers, bold foliage, fragrant. I like 'The Rocket' and 'Desdemona'.
Lobelia, cardinal flower	red	3–4'	summer	N	sun to shade	Bright red color, good for moist shade.

Name	Color	Height	Bloom time	Scent Y/N	Light	Comments
Lychnis, campion	pink	1–2'	summer	N	sun	Soft-textured, gray, hairy foliage. Bright flowers, long-blooming, reseeds.
Mertensia, Virginia bluebells	blue	18"	early spring	Y	partial shade–shade	Beautiful clear blue color, good with spring bulbs. Foliage dies back by early summer.
Nepeta, catnip	lavender to blue	1–3'	summer	Y	sun	Aromatic plants, good foil for brighter plants. Try 'Blue Wonder' and 'Six Hills Giant.'
Oenothera, evening primrose	yellow	1–3'	summer	Y	sun	Fragrant, large group of plants, some invasive.
Paeonia, peony	white/pink/red	1–3'	early summer	Y	sun	Cut flowers, long-lived, low-maintenance plants. Some have nice fragrance.
Perovskia, Russian sage	blue	3–4'	late summer and early fall	Y	sun	Graceful texture, silvery foliage and stem, drought-tolerant. Pinch back early in season to encourage bushiness.
Phlox, border phlox	many	2–4'	summer–early fall	Y	sun–shade	Fine garden plants, fragrant, cut flowers, many useful kinds.
Physostegia, obedient plant	white/pink	2–3'	late summer to fall	N	sun–partial shade	Easy, long-blooming, cut flowers, can be invasive.
Platycodon, balloon flower	blue	2'	summer to early fall	N	sun–partial shade	Long-blooming, easy, low-maintenance, long-lived.
Polygonatum, Solomon's-seal	white	2'	late spring	Y	partial shade–shade	Excellent foliage accent plant, one variegated form. Easy, no-maintenance plant to hide bulb foliage.
Polygonum, fleeceflower	pink/red	2–3'	early summer into fall	Y	sun–partial shade	Some invasive, long-blooming, long-lived, easy maintenance. 'Superba' and 'Darjeeling Red' should be tried.
Primula, primrose	various	6"–2'	spring	Y	partial shade	Old garden favorite, some fragrant.
Pulmonaria, lungwort	blue/pink	12"	early spring	N	shade	Leaves spotted with white, very early bloom, reseeds, good with spring bulbs. I have grown 'Mrs. Moon,' 'Sissinghurst White,' and 'Roy Davidson.'
Rheum, rhubarb	white/red	5–10'	summer	N	sun–partial shade	Related to edible rhubarb, huge, bold-textured plants, unusual.

Plant	Flower color	Height	Bloom time	Native	Light	Notes
Rudbeckia, black-eyed susan	yellow	2–6'	summer	N	sun	Large group of useful, bright colored flowers, good cut flowers. 'Goldsturm,' 'Herbstonne,' and 'Goldquelle' are worth trying.
Salvia, sage	blue/purple	1–3'	spring through summer	N	sun	Some have aromatic foliage, best if spent flowers removed. 'Blauhugel,' 'East Friesland,' and *hematoides* 'Indigo' are nice.
Sanguinaria, bloodroot	white	10"	early spring	N	shade	Early, pure white color, great no-maintenance shade plant, slowly spreads. Nice with spring bulbs.
Scabiosa, pincushion flower	blue	1–3'	early to late summer	N	sun	Good cut flowers, long-blooming if deadheaded. 'Butterfly Blue,' 'Alba,' and 'Fama,' are dependable.
Sedum, stonecrop	white/yellow/pink	2"–2'	spring–fall	N	sun	Butterflies love them, drought-tolerant, low-maintenance, need well-drained soil, many excellent varieties for the garden.
Solidago, goldenrod	yellow	1–3'	late summer and fall	N	sun	Do *not* cause hayfever, great cut flowers, interesting form.
Stachys, lamb's-ears	pink	1–2'	summer	Y	sun	Woolly, silver-haired-covered leaves, sweet scent, good cut flowers, combines well with others, spreads fairly quickly.
Tiarella, foamflower	white	12"	late spring	Y	partial shade–shade	Soft, fluffy-textured flowers, good foliage, combines well with others in shade garden, ground cover plant.
Tricyrtis, toad lily	white/purple	1–3'	fall	N	partial shade–shade	One of the last to bloom in the fall, orchid-like flowers, arching stems when in bloom.
Trollius, globeflower	yellow/orange	1–3'	late spring	N	sun–partial shade	Easy, long-lived, good cut flowers.
Verbascum, mullein	yellow/pink	3–5'	summer	N	sun	Some have bold, white, woolly foliage, reseed, "must-have" texture. Well-drained soils a must, strong vertical effect when in bloom.
Veronica, speedwell	white/blue	1–3'	early to late summer	N	sun–partial shade	Long-flowering, excellent plants. 'Sunny Border Blue,' 'Icicle,' and 'Crater Lake Blue' are good ones.
Veronicastrum, Culver's root	white	3–5'	summer	N	sun–partial shade	Excellent vertical effect, good for late flowers, butterflies love it.

❂ I purposely include a few ornamental grasses, *Rudbeckias*, and cone-flowers (*Echinacea*) because their foliage or seedheads remain standing long after frost claims them in the fall. Their tan-brown colors and textures add interest to dull winter landscapes. There are many other perennials that contribute winter interest and should be considered for areas visible from indoors.

❂ If your Enabling Garden experiences very cold winters include only the very hardiest container plants, ones that will survive virtually aboveground. The larger the container and the warmer your climate, the longer the list of appropriate container perennials. Peonies, yarrow, and hosta are some of the many that will do just fine. Chives, one of the toughest, will survive completely exposed in a 6-inch pot!

❂ Among tall perennials, I look for ones that can stand up on their own without staking. First of all, staking is extra work I don't need when there are plenty of tall plants that don't need it. Second, visible stakes are too distracting from the plants, in my view, but *invisible* stakes are dangerous. I have poked myself in the eye with the common bamboo stake dyed green to be invisible. These are particularly dangerous to people with visual impairments. Unless the stakes are large and tall enough to be visible, like large tomato stakes, I feel you should avoid them.

In my rather large garden, I have enjoyed the plants in the following list, which is by no means inclusive. There are many, many other perennials to try.

Ornamental Grasses

This group of plants has become very popular of late in this country, and deservedly so. True grasses, sedges, and bamboo are often grouped together for the purpose of discussion because their similar grasslike appearance creates the same effect in the garden, namely, soft, feathery texture that lends a unique contrast to other plants. While there are several ornamental grasses generally used as annuals, depending upon the severity of your winters, most are perennials. They are generally very tough, hardy plants that, once established, are drought-resistant, low-maintenance, and trouble-free, providing an extremely long season of interest in the landscape.

Grasses provide movement and sound as they rustle in the slightest breeze, appealing to our senses beyond sight. They can find a niche in any garden, from the formal setting to a more natural garden where grasses reflect or symbolize a grassland, prairie, or meadow. Their soft textures contrast well with the more bold forms, colors, and textures in the garden. They also tend to bind one garden area to another, serving as the backbone of the flower garden as colors quickly shift from plant to plant or location to location as the season progresses.

Grasses contribute their own flowers as well, but they are of softly muted colors and textures that balance the brighter, bolder colors and forms in the garden. They are also very useful in fresh and dried arrangements. Some grasses have fall color and, with their feathery flower plumes

*O*rnamental Grasses

The following short list of good grasses should get you started in this wonderful, carefree, and much larger group of plants.

Annual/grasses—All can be started from seed and do best in full sun.

Briza maxima,
    quaking grass

18 inches, with oat-like seedheads on drooping stems that move in the slightest breeze. Useful in both fresh and dry arrangements.

Coix lacryma-jobi,
    job's-tears

3 feet high, usually grown for its interesting seedpods, which are used for beads.

Pennisetum setaceum,
    white fountain grass

One of my favorite annual garden plants for soft-textured effect. Grows 3 to 4 feet tall. Flower heads are pink, fuzzy, and provide movement in the garden. 'Rubrum' has red foliage and rose-colored flower heads. Work very well with many other annuals and perennials. Foliage tends to cascade over the sides of containers, softening them, too.

Pennisetum villosum,
    feathertop

Easy to grow from seed. Grows about 2 feet tall, beige or tan, with fluffy flower heads.

Perennial grasses—Again, full sun and well-drained soils are generally required. All are hardy in the ground over a wide range of the country, but they may not survive in containers.

Briza media,
    quaking grass

10 to 15-inch tufts of delicate, pendulous, heart-shaped flowers, useful for dried or fresh arrangements.

Calamagrostis acutiflora stricta,
    feather reed grass

4 to 6 feet tall, very upright and erect in all its parts. Flowers appear in June and are held well above the plant, persisting into winter. Excellent drought tolerance.

Carex morrowii 'aureo variegata,'
    variegated Japanese sedge

About 12 inches tall, tolerates partial shade, weeping habit. Variegation lightens up dark places. Sedges, as a rule, tolerate more shade than true grasses.

Chasmanthium latifolium,
    sea oats

This grass resembles bamboo because its leaves stand out at right angles to the stem. Interesting flat, pendulous seedpods appear mid- to late summer and flutter with every breeze. Very shade-tolerant, excellent fresh or dry in arrangements, will reseed in the garden.

Erianthus ravennea,
    ravenna grass

Somewhat similar to less hardy Pampas grass, towards the end of summer it sends up very tall (up to 15 feet) flower spikes, leaves, make rustling sound in the wind. Strong accent or specimen plant.

Hakonechloa macra aureola,
    blue oat grass

Up to 2 feet tall, one of the most beautiful of all grasses that grow best in shade, very graceful, arching stems variegated gold and white.

Helictotrichon sempervirens,
    blue oat grass

Foliage has stiff pincushion effect, strong blue color. Flowers arch gracefully, held well above foliage, and fade to tan color that contrasts well with blue foliage. 24 inches tall.

Miscanthus sinensis,
    eulalia grass

A species with many excellent cultivars ranging from 3 to 7 feet tall. Impressive but graceful soft-textured specimens, some variegated. 'Gracillimus,' 'Morning Light,' 'Silver,' 'Sarabande,' and 'Nikko' are excellent varieties.

Miscanthus sinensis 'purpurescens,' flame grass	Grows to about 5 feet and blooms earlier than most others. White, feathery plumes, purplish color during the summer, good orange-yellow fall color.
Molina caerulea, 'Windspiel'	One of my favorites. Foliage grows about 2 feet tall, with later 7-foot, airy flower spikes arching out and over the plant. These move in the wind for a great sculptural effect, best shown against a plain, dark background.
Pennisetum alopecuroides, fountain grass	Very similar to its annual cousin. Very soft arching foliage and late summer flower stalks up to 3 or 4 feet tall. 'Hamelin' is a shorter and, some feel, a more hardy cultivar.
Spodiopogon sibiricus	Leaves held perpendicular to the stem, giving a strong horizontal effect, Early-blooming flowers appear in July and are a bright, light contrast to the foliage.

---

and foliage, are durable enough to remain standing tall through most of the winter. Their buff-colored, soft-textured elements liven up a barren, snow-covered landscape.

Grasses range in size from the diminutive, 6-inch blue fescue to the towering, 15-foot *Erianthus ravenae,* and everything in between. There is enough color and textural contrast among the grasses to create a very beautiful, and interesting garden with them alone. Some are so effective in the landscape, one makes a wonderful specimen plant all by itself. The best garden performers are clump-forming rather than running, with some being downright invasive monsters that will eat up your entire garden in no time at all.

Grasses are not a novelty, since humankind has used them for food, fiber, and shelter throughout history. We have only recently begun to view them once more for their ornamental character in the garden. They had been used in American Victorian landscapes, but this seemed to fall out of favor. Later in Europe they regained popularity. As we Americans have started to change our gardening habits and desire more low-maintenance plants, ornamental grasses have reasserted themselves, I hope permanently, in our landscapes. They are not commonly used as yet, and chances are, if you put a clump of *Miscanthus* in your yard, you will be the first on your block to introduce your neighbors to this wonderful group of plants.

In your Enabling Garden, you can grow grasses, particularly those treated as annuals, in containers. In the ground-level garden, they offer a low-maintenance alternative for those hard-to-reach areas. They are at their best when we leave them alone. Insects and disease rarely trouble them, so we can leave the poisons in the bottle. Grasses need be cut down to the ground only once a year, in late winter or early spring, to allow for the new fresh growth of the coming year. Their natural, windswept look and textural assets, their ability to rustle in the slightest breeze, and their compatibility with other plants make them an ideal addition to the Enabling Garden.

Vines

Vines are an important group of plants for your Enabling Garden because they make use of all those vertical structures and elements you learned how to build earlier! Vines include annuals, perennials, and woody plants. They must either find support on which to climb or be supported by being tied to a garden structure. With this support, vines bring themselves within your reach for you to tend, harvest a crop or simply appreciate the intricacies of a flower or a leaf. For pure ornamentation, vines offer many low-maintenance alternatives that soften structures or walls, provide screening, and give quick overhead shade when allowed to ramble over an arbor or garden archway.

You should train grapes, kiwi, and other vining fruit plants to a trellis system, keeping them within reach of any gardener so that harvest is easy. Beyond this, I usually limit my vine choices to those that are self-clinging and require at most only minimal pruning, because I have located the other vines in my landscape in places where they will ultimately get be-

---

Vines

Name	Comments
Woody and Perennial	
Akebia quinata, five-leaf akebia	Excellent foliage
Campsis radicans, trumpet creeper	Midsummer flower
Clemetis spp., clematis	Many varieties, good flowers
Hedera helix, English ivy	Good groundcover and climber
Hydrangea anomala 'petiolaris', climbing hydrangea	Very attractive
Lonicera, spp., honeysuckle	Long-blooming, sweet-scented flower
Parthenocissus quinquefolia, Virginia creeper	Good, dependable vine, excellent fall color
Parthenocissus tricuspidata, Boston ivy	Self clinging, good fall color
Polygonum aubertii, silver lace	Fragrant flower
Annual	
Aristolochia dolor, Dutchman's pipe	Unusual flower
Asarina barclaiana, maurandya	Long flowering season
Cobaea scandens, cup-and-saucer vine	Unusual flower
Cucumis sativus, cucumber	Edible fruit
Dolichos lab-lab, hyacinth bean	Beautiful flower, edible purple seedpod
Ipomoea × multifida, cardinal climber	Great texture, flower
Ipomoea quamoclit, cypress vine	Great texture, flower
Lathyrus spp., peas	Many varieties, edible vegetable
Passiflora spp., passionflower	Unusual flower
Phaseolus coccineus, scarlet runner bean	Flaming red flower
Phaseolus vulgaris, pole (garden) beans	Edible seedpod
Thunbergia alata, black-eyed Susan vine	Flowers have black centers, easy
Tropaeolum majus, nasturtium	Edible flower

yond reach. I also carefully select vines to match the space I want to cover. For example, a wisteria of nearly unlimited growth potential would be impractical for a small archway over a garden gate. You would be forever hacking it back out of the way or keeping it from taking over the house. A shorter-stature climbing rose or clematis makes more sense. Take care as well to avoid vines that tend to reseed themselves, such as *Amphelopsis,* and create unnecessary weeding work. Don't cover structures over patios and walkways with vines that drop messy fruit and leaves that must be swept up. Bear in mind that large, woody vines, like bittersweet and wisteria, need strong support if allowed to get to large size.

Annual vines such as cypress vine, canary creeper, and some morning glories, are excellent alternatives to those permanent ones that may get out of control. At least you know annuals will be killed with the frosts of fall, so you can try something different next year, which a permanent vine just doesn't allow. Potentially growing less than 15 feet, they are ideal choices for small trellis boxes and gardens limited to balconies or rooftops. The vines in the following lists are worth trying.

Herbs

This large, diverse group includes annuals, perennials, and woody plants. Besides their obvious aromatic and flavoring qualities, many herbs are very ornamental, contributing unique color, form, and textural qualities to your garden. In your Enabling Garden, herbs deserve a prominent place. For people with visual impairments, where plant characteristics of scent, taste, and texture should dominate, herbs are a natural choice.

Herbs also offer opportunities for activities beyond the garden:

Enhance your favorite recipe Use fresh herbs in cooking or to make herbal vinegars or a simple garnish of fresh mint or parsley to liven up a special dish.

Make herbal crafts Many aromatic herbs, such as lavender, can be grown, harvested, and dried for potpourri, sachets, scented candles, and hundreds of other uses for gifts or even to be sold at local craft fairs. Harvest and dry herbs for later use in teas, herbal baths, and medicinal purposes (with caution).

These are just a few of the many thousands of ways humankind has used herbs throughout history. By careful selection, such multipurpose plants extend the gardening season throughout the year for both your own enjoyment and that of others.

In the garden, you can combine herbs with other plants or grow them in an herb garden dedicated to this wonderful group of plants. I mix a few herbs throughout my garden. Parsley, for instance, is an excellent ornamental plant. Its curly, ruffled, bright green leaves are a soothing foil to other bright plants. Besides its uses in my own recipes, it is a favorite source of fresh greens for our pet parakeets. Our Southern friends should also be able to grow some of our many common spices, like cloves, that are native to tropical regions.

Most herbs can be grown in containers. In fact, some, like peppermint, are very invasive and should be grown in a container sunk into the ground (with drainage holes) to prevent their roots from spreading or in an above-ground container by itself. Peppermint will even survive winters in containers in the far north.

One group of plants that deserves special mention is the scented geraniums. These are relatives of our garden geranium (*Pelargonium*), which, as you know, is itself very aromatic: Cutting dead blossoms or bruising leaves releases very powerful fragrances into the air and onto your hands. Also treated as annuals, the true scented geraniums have been selected and bred to enhance the variety and quality of their fragrances. There are many "flavors" of these special plants now available, including lemon, apple, and peppermint.

As an added bonus, many of them have variably textured leaves. Some are also spotted, striped or even variegated for added visual interest. Some bloom with beautiful flowers, but most are selected for their fragrance, leaf color, and leaf texture. My personal favorite is the peppermint geranium, with maple-shaped leaves covered with soft, downy hairs that, when brushed against, release their very powerful peppermint scent. Its low-growing or cascading nature makes it excellent for a hanging basket, at the edge of a container, or at the edge of a path, where it can cascade over the side and release its fragrance when brushed against. The fragrances of other herbs are also highlighted through this planting plan.

Besides their beauty value, herbs are easy, undemanding plants. For the most part, they must be grown in full sun and, for best fragrance qualities, without a lot of fertilizer. Growing them on the dry side concentrates their essential oils. Some of the more useful annual herbs include basil, dill, fennel, and parsley. My list of favorite perennial herbs includes catnip (favorite of our feline friends and parakeets, too), chamomile, chives, garlic, lavender, lemon balm, mint, oregano, sage, and thyme.

Shrubs

Shrubs, both deciduous and evergreen, along with trees, will form the framework of your garden. Because of their smaller size, you can grow a greater diversity of shrubs than trees. Shrubs are generally woody plants that will live indefinitely, so they should be a one-time investment—usually a cheaper overall investment than trees, although you will probably use more shrubs. The ultimate size of the shrubs will depend on your climate and soil type, and to a certain extent pruning.

I might as well let it be known right away that I believe pruning should generally be avoided except to remove dead or diseased growth and crossed or broken branches. It might also be good to renew some shrubs that flower only on new growth or to restore old, overgrown shrubs to fresh vigor. However, the unfortunate weekend ritual of turning shrubs into boxes, globes, and other unnatural shapes is really unnecessary.

With proper selection, a shrub should not outgrow its location and should require little or no maintenance. This makes the better ones ideally suited to the Enabling Garden, particularly in locations that are not readily accessible. Some of the tougher ones do well in raised beds and larger containers, even in cold winter areas.

When positioning shrubs in your Enabling Garden, besides taking into account their light, moisture, soil, maintenance, and fertility require-

Good Shrubs

This list is dominated by good, low-maintenance shrubs suitable for wide areas of the country. Some species may have many cultivars superior to the standard.

Name	Height/width (feet)	Hardiness (zones)	Comments
Aesculus parviflora, bottlebrush buckeye	8–12/10–15	4–9	Rather slow-growing, suckering shrub, tolerates partial shade. Compound leaves; yellow fall color. White, bottlebrush-like flowers in mid- to late July, when flowers are rare on shrubs; beautiful in flower.
Aronia arbutifolia, chokeberry	6–10/3–6	4–9	Best noted for brilliant red colors in the fall and persistent ¼-inch, bright red berries, which line the stems most of the winter; birds don't seem to like them. Nice where seen from indoors in winter.
Betula nigra 'Little King', dwarf river birch	8/10	4–9	Dwarf form of tough river birch that exhibits peeling, multicolored bark on older stems; good winter texture and color; stays small; yellow fall color.
Buddleia davidii, butterfly bush	3–15/3–10	5–9	Late summer to frost, tiny, sweetly fragrant flowers borne on 6- to 8-inch panicles; various shades of lavender to purple; many varieties available. Favorite stop of butterflies. Herbaceous perennial in north; excellent for color, fragrance, and butterflies.
Buxus microphylla, boxwood	3–4/3–4	4 (some)–9	Nice, small evergreen shrub requiring little maintenance. Can be shaped to formal effect, but I feel its best left alone. Fragrant, but not showy spring flowers.
Callicarpa japonica, beautyberry	4–6/4–6	5–8	Best feature is unusual tiny, violet berries, which line arching stems in the fall. Dies back to ground in north.
Calycanthus floridus, sweet shrub	6–10/6–12	4–9	Chief attribute is 1½-inch, reddish-brown flowers with very fruity fragrance during May into June; smells like strawberry or apple, variable depending on plant. Try to select in bloom to test fragrance; all plant parts fragrant when crushed. Shade tolerant.
Caryopteris x *clandonensis,* blue mist shrub	2–5/2–5	5–9	Nice blue flowers along the stem on new growth in fall; cut back in late winter to encourage new growth. Treat as herbaceous perennial in north; aromatic in all parts.
Clethra alnifolia, sweet pepper bush	3–8/4–6	3–8	Grows in shade or sun; mid- to late summer spikes of very sweetly scented white flowers borne at ends of branches; golden yellow fall color.
Cornus spp., dogwood	various	2–9	Variably fragrant late spring to early summer; whitish flowers. Many shrub forms available; some, like 'Siberica,' have red stems; others have yellow for a nice winter effect.
Corylus avellana 'contorta,' Harry Lauder's walking stick	3–8/3–8	4–7	Best in winter, when contorted, twisting stems visible. Early spring, pendulous catkins attractive.

Plant	Size	Zone	Description
Cotinus coggygria, smokebush	10/10	5–8	Faded late summer flowers make plant look covered in smoke; very fine texture effect. Some have purplish leaf color in summer; all have good fall color.
Daphne spp., daphne	2–4/2–4	4–8	Extremely fragrant pink-white flowers borne in spring; evergreen foliage. 'Somerset' and 'Carol Mackie' (a variegated form) are good ones.
Fothergilla gardenii, dwarf fothergilla	2–3/2–3	5–8	One of the best! Interesting mid-spring, slightly honey-scented creamy white, fuzzy flowers; brilliant orange to yellow to red fall color. Never gets out of bounds; shade tolerant.
Hamamelis vernalis, vernal witch hazel	6–9/6–9	4–8	One of the first shrubs to bloom in very late winter; fragrant yellow to red flowers bloom along the stem. Excellent golden yellow fall color. Several excellent cultivars available.
Hamamelis virginiana, common witch hazel	15/15	3–8	One of the last shrubs to bloom in the fall, with straplike, fragrant, yellow flowers. Brilliant yellow fall leaf color. Many useful cultivars and hybrids.
Hydrangea spp., hydrangea	3–20/3–20	3–9	Several useful species and many varieties valued for mid- to late summer; large clusters of primarily white, but some species have pink or blue; large and sometimes fragrant flower clusters. "Old-fashioned" favorite.
Ilex, spp., holly	2–20/2–20	4–9	Wide group of mostly evergreen shrubs with bright red winter berries. Requires male and female plants to set fruit.
Itea virginiana, Virginia sweetspire	3–5/3–5	5–9	Upright panicles of sweetly fragrant, white flowers on new growth from June through July. Superb, long-lasting, orange to purple fall color.
Juniperus spp., juniper	various	3–9	Widely adaptable group of evergreen trees and shrubs; many smaller species and cultivars that are extremely useful.
Kalma latifolia, mountain laurel	variable	4–9	Needs acid soil, but where easily grown, produces some of the most beautiful spring flowers, ranging from white to red. Hundreds of cultivars available; evergreen.
Lonicera spp., honeysuckle	variable	4–9	Extremely large group of shrubs and vines valued for sweetly fragrant flowers. Can be invasive in some locations.
Magnolia stellata, star magnolia	to 10/10	3–8	Star-shaped, 3-inch fragrant flowers before leaves. Other shrubby magnolias are also worth growing.
Myrica pennsylvanica, bayberry	5–10/5–10	2–7	Large suckering shrub; tolerant of poor soil. Leaves aromatic when brushed; waxy-coated, gray, $1/5$-inch fruits line stems in winter; wax used for scented candles.
Philadelphus coronarius, mock orange	4–10/4–10	4–8	Sweetly scented, white flowers May into June. 'Minnesota Snowflake' and 'Minneature Snowflake' are good varieties.

Name	Height/width (feet)	Hardiness (zones)	Comments
Picea spp., spruce	variable	2–7	Several valuable, needled evergreen species, of which the dwarf varieties maintain shrubby forms. Useful for year-round color and texture.
Pieris japonica, pieris	3–12/3–12	5–8	White, slightly fragrant, tiny flowers in drooping clusters 3 to 6 inches long. Useful evergreen; many cultivars available; needs acid soil.
Pinus spp., pine	variable	2–8	Very large group of needled evergreens, of which there are many shrubby froms. Useful for year-round color and texture.
Potentilla fruticosa, bush cinquefoil	1–4/2–4	2–7	Small, 3/4-inch flowers cover the shrub over a long period; colors range from red to butter yellow to white. Spider mites may be a problem during dry periods. Many varieties to choose from.
Rhododendron spp., rhododendron, azalea	variable	4–9	Extremely large group of evergreen and deciduous plants; mostly spring, with some summer, flowers; some are fragrant and should be sought out. More varieties of this group available than any other.
Rosa, spp., rose	variable	2–9	Shrub or rugosa types less fussy and disease-prone. Can't beat 'em for color, fragrance, and, with those that set vitamin C-rich hips, winter interest. Watch thorns if visually impaired.
Spiraea spp., spirea	3–6/3–6	3–8	Many useful, midsummer-flowering shrubs; white to pink, depending on type.
Syringa vulgaris, lilac	4–10/4–10	3–7	This and many other species and cultivars noted for strongly fragrant, late spring flowers. Old-fashioned favorite; very long lived. Seek out those resistant to typical late summer mildew.
Thuja spp., arborvitae	variable	2–8	Large, tough group of small- to medium-size evergreens; some low mounds, others narrow and spirelike. Soft, scale-like leaves; some are aromatic when brushed against.
Tsuga spp., hemlock	variable	3–7	Dwarf forms of this soft-textured evergreen are very beautiful plants that should be in every garden where they can be properly grown.
Vaccinium corymbosum, highbush blueberry	4–10/4–10	3–7	Various cultivars are superior to the species; needs acid soil. Known for early summer ripening, blue-black berries loved by humans and animals alike.
Viburnum spp., viburnum	3–20	2–9	An extremely diverse group of excellent garden shrubs. Many with good fall color and very fragrant spring flowers; some have effective and persistent fruit. No garden should be without a viburnum of some type.

ments, you must consider their size. Shrubs are available from 6-inch miniatures to those that could be considered small trees, up to 20 feet tall and as wide. You can easily avoid planting 2 feet from the garden path a shrub that will strive to become 10 feet wide. You can also seek out the dwarf form of a favorite standard-sized shrub that would normally outgrow the space you want it in. This allows you to grow more types in smaller space.

Try to site shrubs that offer winter interest, such as persistent fruit, stem color, and overall form, where they can be seen from indoors, so you can enjoy these characteristics when winter snows keep you peeking out your windows. Locate shrubs with fragrant blossoms or aromatic foliage near paved areas, windows, or porches, where their fragrances are easily carried into your house by breezes. I have a very fragrant viburnum located next to my screened porch; its scent is carried throughout the house.

I also enjoy shrubs that bloom out of the normal spring to early summer season. The bottlebrush buckeye, *Clethra*, and *Itea*, bloom in mid- to late summer, contributing their flowers and fragrances at a time when few other woody plants are in bloom. The witch hazels are another favorite because their fragrant blooms represent both the earliest and latest blooming large shrubs in my area and most other places they grow.

The final characteristic I look for in a shrub is fall color. I think my favorite season is fall, with its cool, sunny days and frosty nights bringing out a rainbow of foliage colors in our trees and shrubs. I feel shrubs offer great opportunities for fall color design in your garden. With their smaller sizes, you can combine them to bring the full range of leaf colors to your yard, from the vivid oranges, reds, and yellows to the muted purples and bronzes. Fall leaf color, along with shrubs whose ripening berries contribute their own range of colors long into winter, can make this time of year as visually stimulating as the more floriferous springtime.

The evergreen shrubs, including the hollies, rhododendrons, and boxwoods, can lend important structure and texture to a garden that otherwise becomes barren during the winter. The next best choices for winter interest are the dwarf and slow-growing conifers.

The dwarf and slow-growing conifers are perhaps my ultimately favorite group of plants, not only because of their size—diminutive compared to their normal-sized cousins, which enables them to be used in the smallest gardens. Their incredible variety of colors add to the normal growing season, and their green shines forth during the winter, when other color is lacking. They are probably the lowest maintenance group of plants, which, once established, need only water during extended dry periods. They are also nearly infinite in form and texture, from the ground-hugging junipers, to soft-needled pines, to weeping spruces, and everything in between. By being more unusual, these can be difficult to find, rare and prized by collectors, and higher priced, particularly with larger sizes, where the grower has many years invested in their care. In spite of this, incorporating one or two highly visible specimens can bring a beautiful new dimension to your garden. They combine particularly well with ornamental grasses, really shining together during the winter. Where winters are long, this is important!

As a lower maintenance alternative to perennials, annuals, and vegetables, shrubs are an important group of plants for any garden. The following list will expose you to some of the better kinds.

Trees

Trees set the tone of your landscape and ultimately, depending upon selection and position, establish patterns of light and shadow. Large trees, as they mature, will slowly transform a sunny site to a shady one. This can be readily seen in older neighborhoods, where the landscape has had an opportunity to mature and the tree canopy is more complete, rather than in new housing developments that have no mature trees at all.

There are many good reasons for having deciduous trees in your landscape. They enhance your property value, shade your home and patio when in leaf, saving air conditioning costs, and, conversely, during the winter let the sun shine in, letting your home take advantage of solar heating. Trees offer food and habitat for wildlife, as well as beauty in their flowers, leaves, bark textures, and branching patterns. Evergreen trees also provide year-round color, screening, and windbreaks, and can serve as a darker background against which colors and forms of foreground plants will be better seen. I also feel planting trees touches people on an emotional level in a unique way. People like to get involved in volunteer tree-planting programs in cities and towns throughout America, as the value of our urban forests has become recognized. Many feel this is because in a way, planting trees gives us a sense of immortality: The trees we properly select and plant today will provide shade for generations to come. Couple this with the fact that a tree will have a positive impact on our environment for many years, and it's easy to understand why we value trees so highly.

Trees not only connect us to the future but to our past as well. All of us probably have some memories of a favorite childhood climbing tree or the swing under the old oak tree at Grandma's house. Trees are important on many levels.

As our yards, particularly in urban areas, get smaller and smaller, tree selection becomes more difficult. You must avoid planting them too near structures that are built too close together in the first place, under overhead wires, or shading the patio of your sunbathing neighbor. Water-seeking or shallow roots can invade plumbing and crack sidewalks and driveways. Urban sites can also limit healthy root growth, due to underground physical barriers or poor-quality, compacted soils disturbed by construction activity. Where space is at a premium, the trend is toward using trees that naturallly mature at smaller sizes without pruning to keep them in bounds. Even then, most of us will be limited to a few trees in our landscape.

This is further complicated by knowledge. As the saying goes, a little knowledge is a dangerous thing. Being a horticulturist trying to trim my list of 50 or so favorite trees down to the half dozen or so for my own half-acre lot was and is particularly agonizing. Seriously, though, a clear list of selection criteria will prevent the far too often-made mistake of planting the wrong tree in the wrong place. This both shortens the lifespan of the tree and wastes the investment in buying and planting it in the first place. Some of the criteria I use when selecting a tree include the following:

- Soil, moisture, and drainage requirements.
- Overall mature size and shape relative to the planting location (avoiding overhead power lines, and so on).
- Hardiness to my climate.
- Strong wood that will not break in storms or with ice and snow loads.
- Not creating a fruit-drop or other litter problem if located near a paved area or pathway.
- Grows fast enough so I might enjoy its shade at a larger size during my lifetime, but not so fast as to be weak- wooded.
- Maintains a good, strong branching pattern and central leader without major pruning, other than to establish shape when young.
- Deep-rooted to minimize need for supplemental moisture and to permit underplanting with shrubs and perennials without serious root competition from the tree. Also important for trees planted in or near sidewalks or other paved areas, to avoid long-term heaving.
- Does not readily reseed itself, creating a weeding problem.
- Generally free of pests and diseases prevalent in my area.
- If evergreen, it is important it not break under snow and ice loads.
- Provides food and nesting sites for birds and other wildlife.
- Good fall color.
- Flowers at a time other than spring, although I concede that many very acceptable trees flower in the spring.
- Persistent fruit that hangs on and remains colorful during the winter, until finally consumed by birds.
- Essentially zero-maintenance, because in the Enabling Garden it may be either planted in an inaccessible place or ultimately grow out of reach to tend.

While these criteria will help you narrow down your own list, there are usually many choices to pick from that will be great in your situation. I personally like to pick from trees either native to my area or those that are perfectly suited to my area, but perhaps more unusual—a way of increasing the diversity of trees in my neighborhood and showing neighbors that something besides the mundane can be grown.

Perhaps my favorite group of small trees is *Malus*, or flowering crab apples. They have been around for a long time, brightening up our landscapes with their late spring pink, white, or red flower displays that literally cover the trees. Recent efforts by breeders have overcome many of the disease and fruit-drop problems associated with the older varieties. Also, breeders have introduced many new forms and sizes that are suitable for just about any location in the landscape, from narrow and columnar crab apples, to small and rounded, to low and spreading. Colorful crab apple fruits now persist well into winter, where repeated freezing makes them more palatable to birds. This single group of plants can be grown over a wide area of the country and effectively meets many of the above criteria.

Fruit Trees and Shrubs

An important offshoot of growing trees and shrubs in the garden is the unique pleasure of raising shrub and tree fruits. You can easily incorporate them into an Enabling Garden of just about any size, including rais-

Good Trees

This short list emphasizes trees with wide geographical application, smaller trees for smaller landscapes, and those perhaps a bit more unusual but very useful and that should be grown to a greater extent.

Name	Height/Spread (feet)	Hardiness (zones)	Comments
Abies concolor, white fir	to 50/to 25	3–7	Wide adaptability; "soft" blue-green evergreen needles; will not tolerate heavy clay soils; can get quite large. 'Compacta' is nice dwarf form.
Acer ginnala, amur maple	15–20/15–20	3–8	Very tough, small, usually multistemmed tree. Fragrant spring flowers; brilliant red fall color. Suitable for containers; can be pruned to size and shape for smaller garden; quick growing when young.
Acer griseum, paperbark maple	30/20	5–7	Slow-growing, small tree. Brilliant orange to red fall color; multicolored peeling bark lends texture, color, and interest when defoliated; position where seen during winter; excellent near patios and decks.
Acer japonicum, A. palmatum, Japanese maples	3–20/3–20	5–8	Extremely varied, from low and weeping to upright and spreading. Foliage generally finely divided, lending soft, featherly texture to garden. Good for containers in warmer areas; often very showy flowers and seeds, and brilliant fall colors, as well; best in partial shade.
Amelanchier spp., juneberry	25/15	4–7	Multistemmed, small tree or large shrub. White midspring flowers; small fruits ripen in June and are edible, but birds love 'em too; orange to red fall color, with interesting branching pattern.
Betula nigra, river birch	90"/6	5–9	Soft, textured effect in landscape; fast-growing, tolerant tree; chief attribute is peeling and multicolored bark even when young. 'Heritage' is a good cultivar, as well as 'Little King,' a 10 × 10-foot dwarf. Tolerates wet areas; single or perhaps best as multistemmed tree; resists birch borer.
Cercis canadensis, redbud	20–30/20–30	4–9	Quick-growing, wide-spreading, small tree; jagged branching pattern interesting. Pink to magenta flowers on bare branches in midspring; yellow fall color. Short-lived as trees go, at about 20 to 30 years.
Chamaecyparis spp., false cypress	dwarf to over 100	4–8	Very diverse group of evergreens; dwarf forms make the best garden plants. Wide range of textures and colors; liven up winter landscapes.

Name	Zones	Size	Remarks
Chionanthus virginicus, white fringe-tree	4–9	20/20	Small, spreading, slow-growing tree or large shrub; widely tolerant of soils. Late to leaf out in spring; fragrant, pendulous clusters of soft-textured flowers; blue-black "olives" on female plants in fall.
Cladrastis lutea, yellowwood	4–8	to 50/to 40	Very adaptable, low-maintenance, medium-size tree; upright arching branching habit. Compound, dark green leaf turning yellow in the fall; pendulous, 15-inch-long clusters of white, fragrant, pearlike flowers in early summer; attractive smooth, gray bark.
Cornus spp., dogwood	3–8	5–30/5–40	Large group of suitable small trees and shrubs; flowering dogwood (*Cornus florida*) perhaps best known. Some of the shrub types have red or yellow stems, interesting against snow. Most have spring-blooming, fragrant flowers; tree forms have low, spreading, horizontal branching habit; most have significant fall color.
Crataegus phaenopyrum, Washington hawthorn	3–8	20–30/20–30	One of the toughest trees, with sharp thorns. Fragrant, late spring blooms followed by bright red fruit in October, persisting to March or April; beautiful against snow.
Halesia carolina, Carolina silverbell	5–9	30/30	Chief attribute is four-petaled, fragrant bell-shaped flowers, borne in clusters for up to 2 weeks in the spring. Tolerates some shade.
Juniperus virginiana, eastern red cedar	2–8	variable	Very diverse group of tough evergreen plants; prostrate and dwarf forms useful as ground covers; variable colors and textures; widely used.
Koelreuteria paniculata, golden-rain tree	5–9	35–35	Moderately fast-growing, rounded tree; best in full sun but tolerates shade; very tough and adaptable. Fragrant, 12-inch-long clusters of small, yellow flowers appear during June and July, which is unusual for trees. Flowers followed by clusters of 1-inch balloon-like seedpods that persist into winter.
Magnolia spp., magnolia	5–9	10–50/10–50	Large group of *generally* early-spring-flowering trees. Large, mostly fragrant, white to purple blooms (before leaves); yellow fall color. Smooth bark; spreading branches.
Malus spp., flowering crab apple	3–8	variable to 30/50	Large group of generally white, pink, or red, midspring-flowering trees. Smaller ones good for small landscapes; varying habits suitable for wide locations; quite tolerant, tough trees. Best ones resist diseases and have persistent fruit well into winter. 'Adams,' 'Donald Wyman,' and 'Professor Springer' are good ones.
Nyssa sylvatica, black gum	4–9	40–50/30–40	Brilliant flame fall color and horizontal branching pattern chief attributes; glossy green leaves in summer and small dark fruits fed on by birds; needs slightly acidic soils.
Picea spp., spruce	2–7	variable to over 100	Widely variable group of needled evergreens; many dwarf forms useful in smaller gardens; intolerant of extreme heat and drought.

Name	Height/Spread (feet)	Hardiness (zones)	Comments
Oxydendrum arboreum, sourwood	20–30/20	5–8	Superior small, flowering tree; must have acid soils and be kept evenly moist. Unusual midsummer, fragrant, white blooms; vibrant scarlet fall color, with fruits persisting into winter.
Pinus spp., pine	variable to over 100	3–8	Very diverse group of soft-textured, needled evergreens; many different dwarf forms available. Good for texture and winter effect.
Prunus maackii, amur chokecherry	to 40	3–6	Requires well-drained soil. Spring white flowers in clusters of 10 or so; best attribute is strikingly shiny brown to cinnamon colored bark.
Quercus spp., oak	to over 100, with similar spread	3–9	Large group of generally tough-wooded, long-lived trees. Produces acorns, useful to wildlife but could be litter problem. Adaptable to many soil types; most are deep-rooted, permitting underplanting; most are slow-growing, ultimately very large trees. Some of the best oaks are burr, swamp, white, pin, shingle, and red; many have good fall color.
Syringa reticulata, Japanese tree lilac	30/30	4–7	Small, rounded-crown tree noted for its early to midsummer, large, creamy white panicles of very fragrant flowers. Dark, cherry-like, smooth bark interesting, also.
Taxodium distichum, bald cypress	to 150	4–9	Widely adaptable deciduous tree for wet, dry, or compacted soils. It will get very large. Soft, featherlike foliage appears late, turns reddish-brown before dropping in the fall, revealing the very intricate, horizontal branching pattern.
Thuja spp., arborvitae or western red cedar	variable to over 200	2–9	Another diverse and useful group of soft-textured, non-needle evergreens; useful for screening; dwarf varieties suitable for smaller gardens.
Tsuga canadensis, Canada hemlock	variable to over 100	3–7	Very soft-needled evergreen foliage for soft-textured effect in gardens. Many dwarf cultivars that make beautiful garden specimens. Tolerates some shade; intolerant of hot, dry, windy situations.
Ulmus parvifolia, lace-bark elm, Chinese elm	40–50/40–50	5–9	Grows in variable soils from sun to shade; tough plant. Interesting mottled pattern to peeling bark that reveals varying shades of brown.

ing them in containers alone. Other forms of food-raising, including the vegetable garden, are certainly rewarding, but going into your own yard on a crisp, cool, sunny fall day to harvest your own tree-ripened apples is a unique pleasure.

Due to the fact that fruit trees must be tended, protected from birds, pests, and diseases, other animals who will most certainly want to share your crops, and finally harvested, it is important to locate them in accessible areas of your garden, such as near paved areas or in containers on the patio. The more active gardener can locate them in the landscape as any other shrub or small tree. In addition, the plants will need to be of a size that you can reach. Many shrubs, such as blueberries, gooseberries, and currants, are in the 2- to 5-foot range, perfect for ground-level plantings— even for the seated gardener—because they can be easily reached by hand without special tools.

To me, even more exciting are dwarf fruit trees, such as peaches, nectarines, and apples. Depending upon the variety, they can be from just 3 to 7 feet tall and across. The leaf and fruit size stays the same as on a standard variety, only the plant itself stays smaller. Several "dwarfing" rootstocks available to the nursery industry predictably restrict the top growth to sizes more appropriate to a smaller garden—and much more accessible to people with restricted mobility for tending and harvesting than standard-sized fruit trees. That makes them ideal for the Enabling Garden. Using dwarf plants also enables you to control the amount of any one kind of fruit and grow more kinds, with varying harvest times, in less space.

Dwarf fruit trees are very productive for their size but much more manageable. They also produce heavier crops at a younger age than standard varieties, which may take up to 10 years to produce. I plan to have a dwarf apple orchard comprised of older, more flavorful varieties that commercial growers tend to pass up because they don't store or ship as well as the standard golden delicious or McIntosh. Besides, why grow the same ones in your garden that you can get in the store, too? Try something different. The North American Fruit Explorers (see Sources of Help) are an excellent source of information on both dwarf trees and more obscure varieties. They sponsor grafting workshops around the country, where you can learn to create your own custom varieties. Some nurseries and hobbyists graft several varieties on the same plant. Many excellent references are also available to guide you through the steps of raising quality fruit in your garden.

*E*njoy Your Garden Collection

In your Enabling Garden, the "rules" of plant selection are really the same as any other garden, bearing in mind your individual interests, design style, and climate, so you pick plants appropriate to your area. All plants stimulate the senses, some more than others. If you lack certain senses, select plants that especially stimulate those that remain. Plants requiring higher maintenance and tending must be of a size and location accessible to you, no matter what your mobility restrictions.

Beyond this, just about anything goes. This chapter, hopefully, has stimulated some new ideas for your garden. Rather than be biased in favor of one Midwesterner's attitudes toward his Enabling Garden plants, you must seek out references appropriate for your location. The plant lists for Florida are much different than those for Illinois. Developing a list of your own criteria will be worth the investment in time and effort. The death of some plants is natural and inevitable in the garden, especially if you challenge the norms (whatever they are), but there is a limit! Proper plant selection keeps this aspect to the level of being an inevitable part of learning, rather than a source of endless frustration. The bottom line is, grow what you enjoy and is rewarding for you. If you accomplish this, everything else the Enabling Garden has to offer will follow in due course.

The Design:
Putting It All Together

You have learned about your abilities and limitations, the Enabling Garden structures that accommodate your needs, the tools that help adapt you to the gardening activities you want to do, and some guidelines for selecting a palette of plants to try. That's a lot of information that you are now challenged to arrange in a functional, practical, and aesthetic design that creates a safe, comfortable environment.

Sources of Design Ideas

While this chapter cannot hope to make you a professional garden designer or landscape architect, it will help you begin to think like a professional and compile the useful information that a professional would when analyzing your situation. This chapter outlines the basics that can help you either design the garden yourself or more effectively interact with professional garden designers. The one who must ultimately be pleased with the garden is you.

When designing your Enabling Garden, you may wish to consult a licensed landscape architect, who has expertise in the design process and can help you arrange your various lists of wishes into an aesthetic arrangement. There are landscape architects who design only, those who design and build, and those who serve as project managers with several subcontractors. The scope of your plans will help you decide on the level of help you need.

You should consult a licensed landscape architect (LA) for any of the following reasons.

 If your plans are more complex or require a large budget, errors can be expensive. An LA is experienced with projects of this nature.

❂ If you lack the ability to gather information for a base plan, an LA will have the equipment to accurately identify the existing features of your site.

❂ An LA will be most familiar with local building codes, locations of utilities, and construction easements. An LA may also help you articulate a rationale for a variance (a change in existing codes) needed to provide better access for a person with a disability.

❂ If you lack the organizational or creative skills to articulate the plan of your dreams, LAs are in part artists who, with their special training, can arrange all the necessary and desired components into an aesthetic as well as functional plan.

Thelma E. Honey uses intensive gardening methods that keep plants closely spaced. By allowing plants only enough room to reach maturity, weeds find little room, moisture is conserved, and she spends less time cultivating.

- ☼ If contractors will build certain parts of your garden, blueprints may be required to give them accurate construction specifications. These are best done by a professional.
- ☼ At a minimum, you may want to consult with an LA for a couple of hours to pick each other's brains to establish the best plan for you.

I do feel, however, that the profession of landscape architecture is only just beginning to accommodate people with mobility limitations in the garden. You will need to give the LA a great deal of direction based on what you know about your abilities. The recent Americans with Disabilities Act has encouraged designers to learn accessible design in outdoor environments, but the Enabling Garden, where we actually want to get our hands dirty, is another story. Try to find individuals who have at least had experience designing projects that accommodate everyone, such as at agencies serving people with disabilities, retirement communities or other housing for older adults, and public parks and other spaces designed for universal access. Such an LA will be the most sensitive to your needs.

Another factor to bear in mind when interacting with landscape architects is that their education and reference books express general dimensions for accessible designs in terms of legal minimums or maximums, or dimensions that are optimum or universally accessible and as such accommodate as much of the public as possible. Such standards may apply to slopes, path widths, table heights, and so on. The information you supply about your specific needs will give the *best* measurement for *you,* so don't hesitate to use a tape measure to *customize* the design to *your* needs. This information will affect almost every phase of the garden plan.

The do-it-yourselfer can consult the hundreds of **books, videos, and adult education classes** devoted entirely to garden design. They might take you through a detailed, step-by-step process that results in the best combination of materials, style, and arrangement for your location, tastes, and planned activities. They might guide you through the process for a specific style, such as a Japanese garden, a natural garden, or an herb garden. Many of these will reflect the tastes and convictions of the authors, which may or may not be appropriate for your needs and climate. Any source of garden design information, however, is full of useful ideas to help you stretch your imagination. You will be encouraged to try materials, structures, and plants you may be unfamiliar with and that may be more interesting or practical in the long run. I have listed some of the easiest books to use among the Sources for Help.

Other excellent sources of ideas will be found **all around you**. As you travel through your neighborhood, town, and region, take note of garden features you like. A particular paving material, fencing style, or plant combination may catch your eye.

Public gardens are perhaps some of the best sources. They often display many garden styles, interesting structures, and greater diversity of plants than you would normally find in one place. Many are designed by the best landscape architects in the world and reflect locally appropriate, and available construction materials and techniques. The diverse plant selections on display will also reflect those suitable for your climate.

Professionally designed landscape settings display the most effective combinations.

Most public gardens have libraries, offer classes to the public, and have dedicated staff whose job it is to help you with your home gardening questions. In addition, many public gardens have research programs that, in part, evaluate new, unusual, and exotic varieties of plants collected from all over the world. These efforts attempt to increase the variety of plants that can be grown successfully in the local region and preserve endangered species for future breeding materials. I mention this because many experimental plantings, incorporated into plant displays for evaluation, may ultimately prove to be unsuitable or inappropriate for your garden because they are weedy, insect- and disease-prone, or not hardy. Maybe the little plant you see will quickly grow into an out-of-place monster. So if you see something unusual or interesting, try to make inquiries about it. Extensive records are usually maintained and willingly shared with the public. On the whole, you can usually depend on what you see. Simply remember, however, that seeing a plant that appeals to you does not mean that it is right for your yard.

Another good source of do-it-yourself help are **kits** that allow you to arrange and rearrange cutouts of the various components of your garden on a printed grid drawn to scale. Without drawing and redrawing, you can easily change your design by moving the made-to-scale cutouts of plants, borders, fences, walls, paved areas, and more to different locations on the drawing board until you create the perfect design for you.

There are **computer programs** that produce full-color, three-dimensional visualizations of your house and property, incorporating possible structures and plants into the design so you can actually see what it will all look like. Most of these programs will even show you how the trees and shrubs will look at planting, at different times of the year, and at various stages of maturity, so you can avoid planting the little juniper under the living room window that in 5 years will entirely block it.

Computers can be very helpful, but I feel designing your own garden is one of the most satisfying creative processes there is. Beyond the practical arrangement of the structural elements, you are working with living things that change over time in partnership with nature. Having a computer do it for me would ruin the opportunities to learn from failure, try something new, truly feel pride in assembling an attactive raised-bed planting using unusual plants that I tracked down, and gain the satisfaction of taking advantage of tiny, warm microclimates in my yard to grow something that normally would not survive my winters.

Perhaps the best sources of ideas and information specifically regarding Enabling Gardens are the increasing number of public gardens and organizations and facilities that serve older adults and people with disabilities, with either **horticultural therapy programs or exhibits on enabling garden** techniques. The Chicago and Denver botanic gardens have extensive enabling garden demonstrations staffed by registered horticultural therapists, as do many other programs across the country. Locate those nearest you by contacting the American Horticultural Therapy Association. These programs use many different techniques and designs for making gardening accessible to all and are very willing to share their innovations.

Design Preliminaries

No matter what techniques and tools you use to plan your garden, there are certain basic procedures every designer should follow to some degree to result in the plan you want with the detail you need. The following sections will first help you plan for the various structural components, including raised beds, other plant containers and paving, because such hard features may dominate the overall plan. Plants will be represented conceptually and by category, such as just "Tree," "Shrub," "Perennials," "Vegetables," rather than with specific names. That way, you can use plant lists specific to your location, needs, and climate, and the general designs illustrated are transferable to any location.

Developing a plan on paper is essential because it is easily changed as much and as often as you want. You will ultimately save a great deal of effort and money by avoiding expensive mistakes first discovered on paper. This is most important if your Enabling Gardens will be more complex. If all you desire is a few accessible containers on an existing patio, perhaps a drawing isn't necessary. A paper plan will be essential, though, if you will engage others to build the garden, with detailed drawings serving as their instructions.

In the Enabling Garden, depending upon your degree of mobility, the hard structures may dominate because of the paving required and the necessity of raising the soil to a comfortable working height through containers, raised beds, or other options. These and other functional components must be considered as higher plan priorities than any other except budget. Without the necessary enabling components, the garden will be a useless source of frustration because even its aesthetics will decline if you can't maintain it.

Perhaps at this stage you may want to review your list of Enabling Garden needs to be sure you are taking everything into consideration.

Equipment

Before setting out on the design process for your garden, you may want to gather a few items that will assist you in transferring your ideas to paper. These materials are not absolutely essential, because even a well-considered, sketchy plan is a great deal more useful than none at all. However, the more accurate and detailed your plan is, the more useful it becomes, particularly if you engage contractors to build the structural components or position and plant difficult-to-move larger trees and shrubs. Such garden components need to be accurately communicated. Some useful tools include the following.

Graph paper You can purchase this in various scales from art supply stores. The lines should match the scale you choose for your plans. Hold the paper in place on a table, a piece of Masonite, or a portable drafting board using **drafting tape** which looks like masking tape, but is easily removed without tearing the paper. **Vellum** is a special, light-sensitive paper for transferring and copying original drawings to blueprints. I suggest, however, that if your plan is complex enough to require blueprints, you should consider a professional to do the drawing.

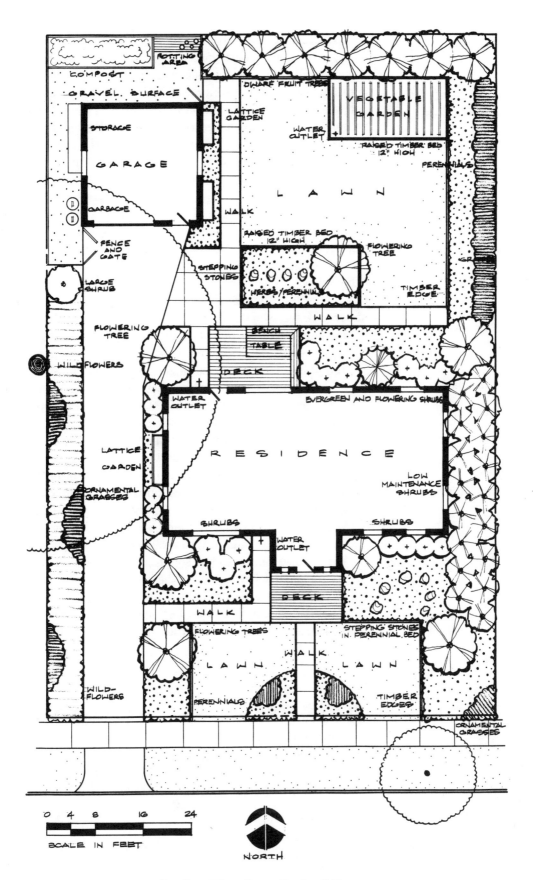

COMPOST
POTTING AREA
GRAVEL SURFACE
STORAGE
GARAGE
GARBAGE
FENCE AND GATE
LARGE SHRUB
FLOWERING TREE
WILDFLOWERS
LATTICE GARDEN
ORNAMENTAL GRASSES

LATTICE GARDEN
DWARF FRUIT TREES
VEGETABLE GARDEN
WATER OUTLET
RAISED TIMBER BED 12" HIGH
PERENNIALS
L A W N
WALK
RAISED TIMBER BED 12" HIGH
FLOWERING TREE
STEPPING STONES
HERBS / PERENNIALS
TIMBER EDGE
W A L K

BENCH
TABLE
D E C K
WATER OUTLET
EVERGREEN AND FLOWERING SHRUBS
R E S I D E N C E
LOW MAINTENANCE SHRUBS
SHRUBS
WATER OUTLET
SHRUBS
DECK

WALK
FLOWERING TREES
STEPPING STONES IN PERENNIAL BED
WILD-FLOWERS
L A W N
WALK
L A W N
PERENNIALS
TIMBER EDGES
ORNAMENTAL GRASSES

0   4   8   16   24
SCALE IN FEET

NORTH

Garden Plan for a Retired Person

Matthew Frazel, HTR, Horti-cultural Therapy Supervisor at the Chicago Botanic Garden, offers the following unique idea. "Plant birdseed (sunflowers, millet, milo, and wheat) at the beginning of the summer. These plants in a birdseed garden make an attractive display that produces seeds. This simple activity provides materials that link the seasons: a birdseed garden in summer, harvesting and mixing seed in fall, and making pinecone bird feeders in winter."

Architect's or engineer's scale This fancier version of the ruler enables you to convert actual garden drawings to the scale you are using in your plan. For example, the 1/8-inch to 1 foot ratio, commonly used by architects, would mean that a raised bed 4 feet wide would be drawn 1/2-inch wide on paper. This architect's scale also uses various other common fractions of an inch to convert dimensions, such as 1/4-inch, to 3/8-inch, and 1/2-inch to 1 foot. An engineer's scale, on the other hand, uses a system based on 10, with such ratios as 1 inch to 10 feet, and 1/10-inch to 1 foot. The two scales work equally well when converting measurements in the garden to paper.

The scale you select should enable you to easily show detail without needing very large paper. You should especially use a professional scale if your drawing must be interpreted by others. Using a 1/4-inch to 1-foot scale, the typical 75 x 150 foot lot should fit on a piece of paper 24 x 48 inches, allowing plenty of room for notes in the margins. Separate drawings of smaller areas, like a deck plan or the layout of a perennial border, may require scales up to 1/2-inch to 1 foot to show the detail you need.

Medium hardness pencils with a high-quality erasers.

Clear plastic 45 degree triangle to help you draw accurate angles.

Templates These are used to accurately draw circles, squares, rectangles, and other shapes of varying sizes. There are also some that represent trees and shrubs, fences, and other landscape components. You could also use a **compass** for drawing circles.

I also use a **flexible curve** which when bent holds its shape. It has one flat surface that provides edges against which you can draw curved lines, indicating edges of planting beds and other informal or organic shapes.

Tracing paper Once you've positioned existing features, such as your house and driveway, on graph paper, you can readily trace them as often as you wish. Especially when you sketch very basic ideas and need several quick copies of your base plan, you will find tracing paper very useful.

You can also purchase more sophisticated architectural tools, such as a **T-square** and **drawing table** but the preceding basics alone will enable you to make very useful drawings. Even if you can't draw at all, think about the following design steps. Listing needs and any other important information is very useful when articulating your ideas to those who will help you or the professional.

*T*he Five Essential Steps of Garden Design

All professional garden designers and landscape architects follow five steps when designing a garden. These steps, in turn, can be further broken down into various layers of considerations that require increasing levels of technical knowledge and artistic ability. The five steps:

1. Base information
2. Site analysis
3. Checklist of needs and wants (wish list)
4. Concept plans
5. Final design

Each successive step builds on the information gathered in the previous ones, resulting in perhaps several final designs from which to choose.

Base Information

The base plan supplies the very basic information from which the plan will emerge. At this stage all important existing features of the site are considered and drawn to scale on paper. Much of the base information you need is usually shown on the plat of survey for your property, which is made at the time of purchase of your home or anytime it changes owners. If lost, copies should be available from your town's planning department. A plat accurately shows property lines and dimensions, position of the house on the property, and any permanent structures, such as garages and driveways. It should also indicate utility easements and service lines.

If a plat is not available, you will probably need to hire someone to measure your property, unless you have the mobility to do it yourself. Existing trees and their shade lines, planting beds, and other features, such as rock outcroppings, ponds, and slopes, are also drawn into the base plan. They can be easily located using straight lines off the corners of the house and other permanent structures. Also included are locations of doors, windows, and water sources. All basic information for your site should be transferred to your graph paper, drawn to scale in bold lines that will show through tracing paper.

As shown in the base plan illustration, a 75 x 150-foot, typical quarter-acre is our example of an urban or suburban lot. It has a single-story (we don't like stairs), 3-bedroom, 1½-bath ranch house, with a detached, 1½-car garage and a concrete driveway. It also has a 150-square-foot wooden deck. Short concrete walks connect the driveway and sidewalk along the street to the front and rear doors of the house. This is usually the information you would expect on a property survey, and it should be included on your base plan. Again, all this information may not be needed if, for example, you are only creating a new patio off the rear of the house. Focus only on the area being considered.

Site Analysis

Site analysis builds upon the base plan by evaluating all the inventoried features from several perspectives. It is a written list of bullets that documents judgments and facts about the site. This evaluation also begins to establish both the possibilities and limitations for the site and how existing features have impact on the future design. For example, you probably won't move your house, and your neighbor's tree is an asset. They will effect the final design, as should any governing laws and the overall character of the surrounding neighborhood. Existing walkways that are in bad shape must be replaced, so perhaps you can plan to reroute them or remake them with a better material.

The following examples that may offer insights to your site:

✪ Connecting walks in bad shape need to be replaced—reroute?
✪ Need larger paved areas for wheelchair user, added patio, or larger deck?

- Deck is well-placed and in good shape?
- Slope will need to be corrected.
- Neighbor's tree casts shade on deck in afternoon but allows good morning sun.
- Only one large place in backyard that gets sun all day—possible vegetable garden.
- Bad views of neighbor's trash cans or nearby building.
- Old Victorian character of house, neighborhood—preserve plants and style of period.
- Village ordinance says you must have a grass front lawn of X square feet.
- Laws prohibit use of certain invasive plants.
- Prevailing wind direction?
- Use garage and house walls for vertical gardening.

The point here is that the more angles you view a site from, the more considered the final plan. The site analysis results from careful consideration of the site and its features from the legal, natural, cultural, and aesthetic perspectives.

The **legal aspects** encompass easements, building setbacks, and building codes that dictate how and where permanent structures must be built on your property. Again, a set of guidelines should be available from your local planning department for projects requiring building permits, giving local construction codes. They can vary greatly from one location to another, even within the same town, so they must be considered carefully.

The **natural components** of the site are things like sun/shade areas, slopes, existing soil conditions, low areas of poor drainage, and predominant wind directions. This information should also be noted for neighboring features that affect your property, such as shade from a neighbor's structure, building, or large tree. This information will begin to define what kind of microenvironments may be exploited, the kinds of plants that can be grown, and how you may need to change to accommodate paving, accessible slopes, structure requirements, and other wishes. These features should also be noted on the base plan, as shown.

The **cultural aspects** of the site are those like the character of the surrounding neighborhood. Are the homes contemporary or older? What sorts of ethnic characteristics are reflected in styles? Is there any historical significance? For example, the landscapes of Colonial Williamsburg are suited to the town's 18th-century character. Cultural aspects will begin to suggest appropriate structure styles, construction materials, and planting design.

Lastly, note the **current aesthetics** of the site. What are its unique features? The 200-year-old oak tree in the neighbor's yard, the attractive weathered wood color of the deck, and your neighbor's fence may be among assets that should be accentuated. Among site liabilities that should be eliminated or screened, are the neighbor's compost pile, a nearby parking lot, and noise from a busy street.

The site analysis is an important source of critical information for the final design. It may also affect the final budget. For example, with a se-

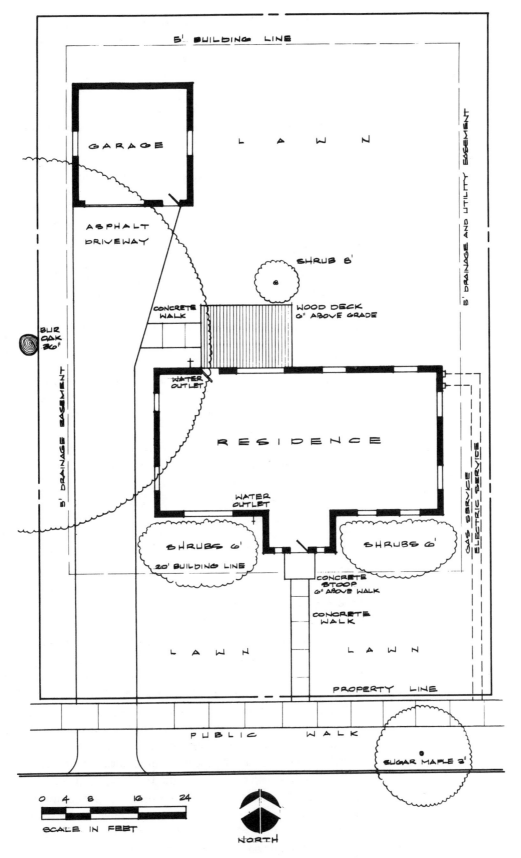

5' BUILDING LINE

GARAGE

L A W N

5' DRAINAGE AND UTILITY EASEMENT

ASPHALT
DRIVEWAY

SHRUB 8'

BUR
OAK
36"

CONCRETE
WALK

WOOD DECK
6" ABOVE GRADE

5' DRAINAGE EASEMENT

WATER
OUTLET

R E S I D E N C E

GAS SERVICE

ELECTRIC SERVICE

WATER
OUTLET

SHRUBS 6'

20' BUILDING LINE

SHRUBS 6'

CONCRETE
STOOP
6" ABOVE WALK

CONCRETE
WALK

L A W N

L A W N

PROPERTY LINE

P U B L I C   W A L K

SUGAR MAPLE 3"

0   4   8   16   24

SCALE IN FEET

NORTH

Base Plan

verely sloped site, it would be both complex and expensive to provide appropriately graded access to those using wheelchairs. This area would better be designed to be inaccessible and low-maintenance, not requiring access.

Checklist of Needs and Wish List

This step is essentially a written list of your requirements and considerations, based on what it is you plan to do on the site. It is also an investigation of possibilities, based on what you wish could be included in the garden. A sample checklist might include things like these:

- Private place to sit
- Minimal slopes
- Place to sunbathe
- Access to as much of the yard as possible
- Vegetable garden
- Compost area
- Large enough lawn for parties
- Plenty of outdoor seating for guests
- Shady place for comfort
- Arbor for vining plants
- Extra paving required for wheelchair user
- Irrigation system
- Don't want any lawn at all because can't mow it
- Automatic irrigation
- Water feature
- Large area for perennials
- Storage space for outdoor furniture
- Privacy from neighbors
- and anything else you think of—now is the time!

Many garden design books offer you long lists of questions you can ask yourself to be sure to consider all possibilities. At this point, you don't want to be concerned with actual sizes and shapes of these needs and wants; you are essentially beginning to define your purposes and priorities. The checklist will also establish some of the structures needed in the garden. For example, if you are a wheelchair user and want a vegetable garden, you need to begin considering some type of raised bed or container garden area, with appropriate surrounding paving for access.

The Concept Plans

This step relies on the information gathered in the previous three steps as you begin to position the checklisted needs and wishes onto the site plan. This is often referred to as the "blob stage" of the design: You are locating the new features by drawing them into rough locations, using blobs as markers. This can be done by laying tracing paper over the site analysis and loosely drawing in the locations of your concepts. Our vegetable garden, for example, must be located in a sunny area of the yard. Because the gardener uses a wheelchair and requires some sort of paving to and around it, it should also be located where paving expenses can be minimized. If mobility isn't a problem, the vegetable garden might be located near the garage, where the tools are stored and the compost area can be hidden behind, being nearer the source of most yard wastes.

This stage of the plan also utilizes the existing features we identified previously that we want to keep, and incorporates appropriate items from the checklist. Places to sit in the shade and sunbathe, in our example, are

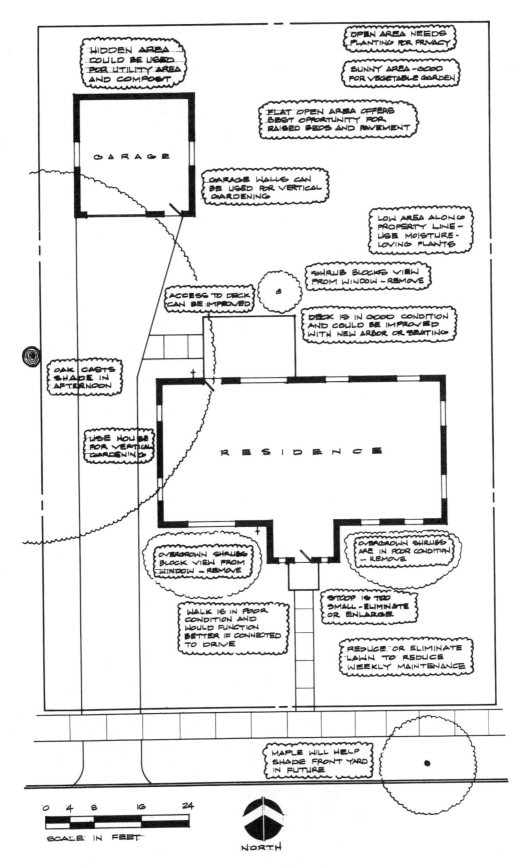

HIDDEN AREA COULD BE USED FOR UTILITY AREA AND COMPOST

OPEN AREA NEEDS PLANTING FOR PRIVACY

SUNNY AREA - GOOD FOR VEGETABLE GARDEN

FLAT OPEN AREA OFFERS BEST OPPORTUNITY FOR RAISED BEDS AND PAVEMENT

GARAGE

GARAGE WALLS CAN BE USED FOR VERTICAL GARDENING

LOW AREA ALONG PROPERTY LINE - USE MOISTURE-LOVING PLANTS

SHRUB BLOCKS VIEW FROM WINDOW - REMOVE

ACCESS TO DECK CAN BE IMPROVED

DECK IS IN GOOD CONDITION AND COULD BE IMPROVED WITH NEW ARBOR OR SEATING

OAK CASTS SHADE IN AFTERNOON

USE HOUSE FOR VERTICAL GARDENING

RESIDENCE

OVERGROWN SHRUBS BLOCK VIEW FROM WINDOW - REMOVE

OVERGROWN SHRUBS ARE IN POOR CONDITION - REMOVE

WALK IS IN POOR CONDITION AND WOULD FUNCTION BETTER IF CONNECTED TO DRIVE

STOOP IS TOO SMALL - ELIMINATE OR ENLARGE

REDUCE OR ELIMINATE LAWN TO REDUCE WEEKLY MAINTENANCE

MAPLE WILL HELP SHADE FRONT YARD IN FUTURE

0 4 8   16   24

SCALE IN FEET

NORTH

Site Analysis

already indicated by the existing sun/shade line on the deck, kindly provided by the neighbor's large oak tree. The notes on the plan should indicate views from within the house, as well as other major viewing directions that you want to improve, create, or totally screen off. Don't be concerned at this stage about accuracy of measurements—many of your blobs may overlap, indicating multiple-use needs or several needs being satisfied by one area. If sunbathing and a vegetable garden are both requirements and there is only one sunny area in the yard, you will simply design into the vegetable area a place to put the lawnchair. I think the vegetable garden is a great place to visit. Besides, while you are there, you will be a living scarecrow as well!

You *must* consider your abilities and your limitations at this point in the plan. Don't locate your frequently visited sunbathing-vegetable area in a remote corner of the yard if your mobility is limited, or you won't use it in the long run. If you use a wheelchair, you must decide what paving is necessary to perform desired tasks or visit certain areas of the property. Inaccessible places should be indicated and later planted with low-maintenance shrub borders for example, which will not require as ready access as the raised vegetable container gardening areas.

In our example, the wheelchair user may want to enlarge the deck or create additional paved patio space and added paths to increase general access and mobility around the yard. This is why the information you gathered in Chapters Two, Three, and Four is so important. The lists you developed there, indicating what structures you will need, must now be accommodated in the design of the garden. As I said before, even if you don't do your own design, this information is invaluable to the designer you select.

The final point I want to mention here is that tracing paper is cheap. Take your time, let your imagination flow, and try to look at possibilities

from fresh viewpoints. Scan books for ideas. Make several different concept plans, because at this point that's exactly what they are—conceptual and easily changed.

The Final Design

Finally, after all the research, conceptualizing, and dreaming, a final plan can be drawn that represents, to scale, the visualization of your ideas. If I have done my job, you will at least be able to articulate your needs and wishes to a professional for a final drawing suitable for construction, if necessary. Of course, if your garden area is limited to an apartment or condominium patio or balcony, such elaborate drawings are not required. Whenever you must rely on others to build or plant the garden, however, the instructions or plans you give them should be as complete as possible. Detailed drawings at a large scale may need to be done for smaller areas, such as perennial borders, decks and patios that may have many containers, and any other area with details too small to illustrate at the existing scale. Additional perspectives showing vertical components like walls, fences, arbors, and other structures that create important growing areas in your Enabling Garden may also be useful. These three-dimensional drawings are very helpful for visualizing how the final plan will appear when constructed.

Indicate accurately both ground-level and containerized planting areas with connecting or any other paving areas. Specific plants should be drawn according to their mature sizes and accurately labeled. You may wish to make several tracings of planting beds to indicate seasonal color or make new plans in the future. When locating plants, keep taller ones to the center or rear of beds to serve as foils for shorter ones. In your Enabling Garden, whatever is necessary to bring plants within reach is appropriate. Placing a taller plant near paving at the front of a border, with blossoms positioned within easy reach of the nose, may be best, as with any plant requiring frequent ATTENTION from a person using a wheelchair.

Several plans have been prepared for our suburban lot that accommodate people with fairly restricted mobility and activity levels. The plantings indicated are still generalized because the location of the garden is Anywhere U.S.A., whereas specific locales each have their own appropriate palettes of plants.

The final design for your Enabling Garden will reflect your physical abilities and limitations. Perhaps all you want or can handle are a few accessible containers on your small apartment patio or balcony, or perhaps a few window boxes on a deck railing. On the other hand, with a bit more desire, time, and energy, your Enabling Garden can be as elaborate as any other garden you will ever see. Most of us will be somewhere in between.

No matter how small or extensive, your Enabling Garden will reflect your individuality and creativity in its layout and in its plants. Your carefully selected structures and tools, and those you may need in the future, will keep you outdoors and active in your garden.

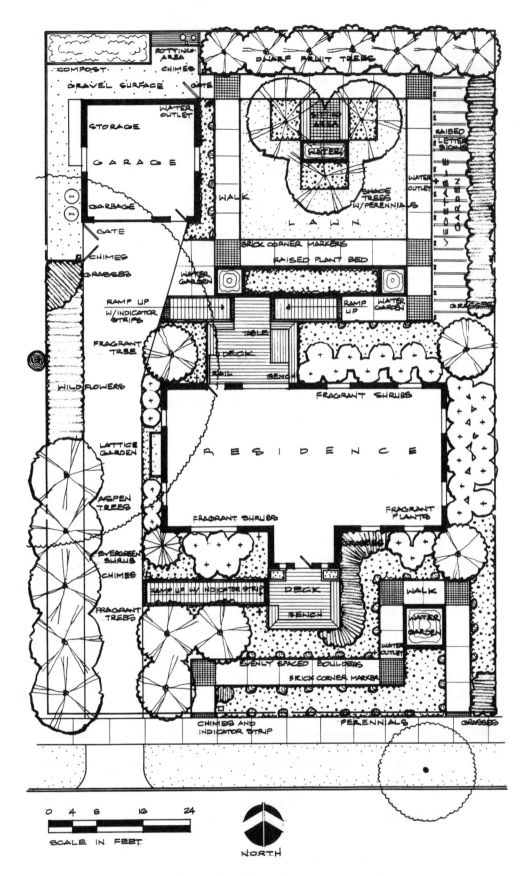

Garden Plan for a Visually Impaired Person

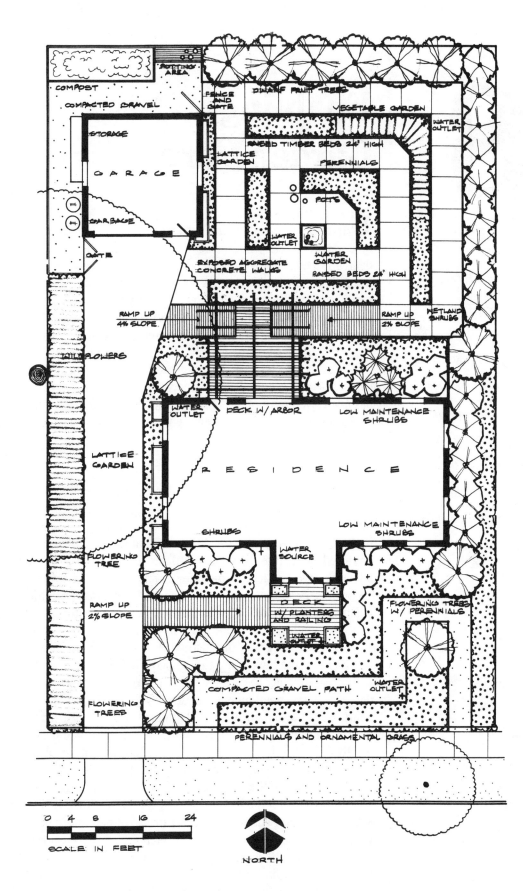

POTTING AREA

COMPOST

COMPACTED GRAVEL

STORAGE

G A R A G E

GARBAGE

GATE

FENCE AND GATE

DWARF FRUIT TREES

VEGETABLE GARDEN

WATER OUTLET

RAISED TIMBER BEDS 24" HIGH

LATTICE GARDEN

PERENNIALS

POTS

WATER OUTLET

WATER GARDEN

EXPOSED AGGREGATE CONCRETE WALKS

RAISED BEDS 24" HIGH

RAMP UP 4% SLOPE

RAMP UP 2% SLOPE

WETLAND SHRUBS

WILDFLOWERS

WATER OUTLET

DECK W/ ARBOR

LOW MAINTENANCE SHRUBS

LATTICE GARDEN

R E S I D E N C E

FLOWERING TREE

SHRUBS

LOW MAINTENANCE SHRUBS

WATER SOURCE

RAMP UP 2% SLOPE

DECK W/ PLANTERS AND RAILING

FLOWERING TREES W/ PERENNIALS

WATER OUTLET

FLOWERING TREES

COMPACTED GRAVEL PATH

WATER OUTLET

PERENNIALS AND ORNAMENTAL GRASS

0 4 8   16   24

SCALE IN FEET

NORTH

Garden Plan for a Wheelchair User

8

Enabling Garden Care

*Martha Straus, HTM, is a horticultural therapist from Pennsylvania. "My favorite idea is the way I rake leaves. Because of my bad back, I can't bend, so I take two rakes and scoop the leaves up together and put them into a cart. It is sort of like a giant pooper picker upper. It is somewhat awkward at first, but really saves on the bending." She also recommends people garden **up,** using long, runner types of vegetables, rather than bush types, and staking them and anything else they can. She also harvests vegetables while sitting on a box. All reduce bending.*

Ultimately, the maintenance of your Enabling Garden will be dictated by its location, size, and design, the plants you have selected, and the degree of perfection you demand. This book is dedicated to illustrating ideas that make gardening easier, but routine maintenance will still be required. There is no such thing as a no-maintenance garden, but you have been shown that the amount of garden maintenance is largely determined by your design, which should be based on your abilities to perform maintenance. Obviously, a larger garden tends to require more work than a smaller one. And a garden dominated by natural or native landscapes will require less work, even on a larger scale, because nature has been given most of the work. I am fortunate that my garden keeps me physically and mentally busy enough to keep it fresh, challenging, and a major source of exercise.

One extremely important point I want to reemphasize here is that as we age, no matter what our *current* abilities, we tend to have less of them. If we live long enough, disabilities will catch up to us. Definitely, not all of our abilities will decrease, and not all to the same degree or at the same rate. What this means in the Enabling Garden, however, is to *plan ahead* in the original design for the addition of more structures, such as paving or raised beds, that we may need later as our abilities decrease. Such adaptations are easier if allowed for during original construction and certainly less expensive, as prices inevitably increase. Additionally, this means perhaps modifying your planting design over time to require less hands-on maintenance while still providing beauty, interest and food.

Using my own case to illustrate this point, I have relied heavily on perennials in the bulk of my garden beds. I also currently have the desire and physical ability to care for them. I have deliberately planned for the day when I will spend more time raising vegetables, and I know the touch of arthritis I have in my hands will gradually worsen, restricting my ability to push my wheelchair and use tools. To accommodate this, I now have mostly mixed borders of perennials, young shrubs, and small trees. As the lower maintenance shrubs and trees gradually mature, they will fill in and eliminate much of the space currently occupied by higher maintenance perennials. Most of the better trees and shrubs are low-maintenance once established. I may still want a pocket or two of perennials here and there for seasonal color in the easiest to reach places, but the amount of day-to-day work will be greatly lessened as the garden matures along with me. At that point in my life, I will concentrate my intensive gardening on paved areas in raised beds near the house, passively enjoying my mixed shrubs and small trees more than expending energy tending them. Of course, you can always quickly convert an area of higher maintenance plants to lower ones by simple replacement. The point here is that the amount of maintenance required in your garden can be just about as flexible as you need.

Given that all gardens do need some routine maintenance—and the Enabling Garden is no exception—the following sections briefly review the major maintenance concerns in most of the country: watering, fertilizing, weeding, pruning and grooming, pests and diseases, and winterizing. The timing of maintenance activities, the pests and diseases you encounter, and the actual duties you perform will all vary with your local climate. By all means, rely on your own lifetime of gardening experience, or seek out others for local information if you move to a new area. If at all possible, maintain a garden journal as a source of information on successes, failures, bloom times of various plants, pest and disease problems and how and when they were handled, and any other information useful to you. A journal is particularly valuable in the vegetable garden, where it really aids in future planning. Taking pictures of your gardens throughout the year provides an excellent record of successful plant combinations, points up plants that should be moved, and most usefully serves as a map of what's where. You can make notes on the backs of the photos, which should each be dated. During the winter, as you plan for next year, this photo record, along with your journal, are probably the most useful planning tools you have. A picture is worth a thousand words that most of us don't have time to write.

*W*atering

As much as I whined about watering in Chapter Five, you may have been tempted to move to Phoenix, landscape with native cactus and succulents, and let nature take care of it all. That's okay, but it won't be long before a pot or two of geraniums will creep onto the patio. You'll sure miss those tomatoes, and before you know it, you need a hose. Actually, once it's all set up to minimize hassle, *some* hand-watering is very relaxing, fun, and a good source of physical activity in even the smallest garden. The following tips should help.

- ✪ Smaller containers dry out more quickly than larger ones. Some may need watering up to twice a day as plants mature and roots fill the containers.

- ✪ Porous clay pots dry out faster than plastic and other sealed surfaces. Clay can be sealed, too.

- ✪ Newly planted trees and shrubs, particularly those that were balled and burlapped, require thorough soaking every week or ten days. Even though rains may keep surrounding soil moist, these new plants will get most of their moisture from within the root ball until a new root system develops. Soaking is best accomplished with a hose near the trunk, set on a slow trickle for up to several hours, depending on the size of the plant.

- Vegetable gardens and most annuals do best with 1 inch of water a week.

- Deep, thorough waterings are much more effective than shallow ones because they encourage deep root systems that use available moisture more efficiently. Water your containers until the water emerges from drainage holes. Note that overly dry, highly organic soils tend to shrink and pull away from the sides of the containers, creating gaps where water simply runs down the sides and out the bottom. This will require successive drenchings, until the soil absorbs enough water to swell up again.

- Group plants of similar watering needs or frequency together, whether they be in the ground or containers. This will save water, time, and energy.

- Established trees and shrubs (planted 3 years or more) should require watering only during excessive drought, and then given first priority. Let the lawn go!

- Plants grown in containers tend to act as umbrellas, actually shedding rain away from the containers if their foliage overlaps the sides. This is an adaptation by plants that delivers water to the newest feeder roots, located around the plant's drip line in nature. They must usually be watered even if it rains.

- Large raised beds can be treated similarly to ground-level gardens because they hold more soil and water.

- Get a rain gauge to measure nature's free water. Don't apply any more tap water than you have to. It's expensive and wasteful.

- Mulch! Mulch! Mulch! Even containers benefit from shallow mulches. Never leave bare soil uncovered: Plant it or mulch it.

Finally, watering to a certain extent has been overdone in American gardens. Let plants tell you when they need it. Many plants take on a dull grayish cast before they actually wilt. Even a *little* wilting will do no harm. Check the soil in containers for dryness before routinely watering. Most plants are pretty resilient and can take a drying out without giving up the ghost. However, those that need consistent moisture, such as most vegetables, should be provided what they need.

*W*eeding

Alas, a weed is simply any plant out of place, or one that we don't want even if it is in the right place. The most important thing is to be able to distinguish the weeds from the good plants. Yes, of course you know which is which, but the best way to weed is to find someone else to do it, and *they* may *not* know which is which. As more unusual plants are grown in our gardens, and as more naturalistic styles of gardening become increasingly popular, such distinctions may become less easy still. Many of our plants, such as Virginia bluebells, bloodroot, and Jack-in-the-pulpit kindly reseed themselves and must be distinguished from less desirable seedling invaders. I pulled many baby Jacks-in-the-pulpit before I knew what they were. Either you or your helper will need some experience or a good teacher to tell seedlings apart, because the best time to pull weeds is when they are small, before they have a chance to flower and set more seed.

Plant labels may be useful here, particularly in a perennial or plant collectors' garden, where there may be a great diversity of plants or many varieties of a single plant, such as daylilies, which are very difficult to tell apart when not in flower. For someone with limited vision, plant labels may be the best way to say "This plant stays." There are many types of unobtrusive labeling systems available. Simple small, white, plastic labels, marked with felt-tip pens with permanent ink, will last about a year.

While I will pull the errant weed if I see it, I usually thoroughly weed my garden only twice a year, once in late spring—in Chicago, around the time the dandelions bloom—and once in late summer. I also time this after a rain so they are easier to pull either by hand or with any of the tools of choice for the job. I elicit help from my wife, and the two of us cover our half-acre yard in a couple of easy-paced hours where we get caught up on each other's busy lives. For us, weeding is quality time.

The best tool to use against weeds in all planting beds is mulch. A fresh layer of mulch does more to suppress weed seeds from growing than any other nonchemical control. The key is *fresh* mulch. As older mulch decays, ironically, it creates an ideal place for weed seeds to germinate.

The lawn is a different story. The best lawn weed suppressant is a good, thick, healthy turf. Take all the steps in your area for a healthy lawn, and most weeds will be choked out. I confess this is one of the very few places I use chemical contols in my garden, because I cannot keep up with digging weeds and have difficulty bending over for lengthy periods. I mix liquid weedkiller in a bottle that can spray a stream. I gradually work my way around the yard on a calm day, playing Quick-Draw McGraw, spot-spraying each weed. Spot-spraying is much better for the environment than broadcasting granular or liquid weedkillers over the entire lawn, where there is also greater risk of damaging shallow tree and shrub roots. Also, some of these chemicals can accumulate in the soil, possibly damaging desirable plants.

Weeds are unavoidable in the garden. You can view this and any garden task as a source of exercise. You can also worry less about a weed or two here and there—so what!

*F*ertilization

Fertilization is also one of the things we gardeners tend to overdo, but in some situations it is very appropriate.

Containers, raised beds, and other frequently watered situations require fertilization, especially in those with soilless mixes (discussed earlier). The frequent waterings given containers and ground-level beds with any fast-draining soils quickly leaches away nutrients that will need to be replaced if the plants are to remain healthy and productive.

The ground-level vegetable and annual gardens are other places that call for especially fertile soil and nutrient renewal because the plants are grown closer together, and, as we remove our harvest, nutrients are rapidly depleted.

Ornamental beds and trees and shrubs, once established, usually do not require supplemental feedings, unless the soil in your area is known to be deficient in something. However, feeding these plants routinely will spur additional growth and vigor. All of my perennials and mixed borders, trees, and shrubs are surrounded with 2 to 5 inches of organic mulch, depending on what I am using for mulch. I have found that, as this material decays, plenty of fertility is released to sustain healthy growth. In fact, some of my perennials indicate overfertilization by producing leggy growth that flops over. Shredded or composted leaves are one of the best sources of nutritional organic mulch. Don't be so fussy about removing plant debris from beds. Unless it is diseased or full of unwanted seeds, leave it lay to decay and contribute to the soil and plant health. Mother Nature doesn't use a leafblower to clean up after herself. This material, left on growing areas along with the mulches, will be nothing but beneficial, providing all the fertility most plants need.

You can also feed lawns organically with some of the newer formulations that supply nutrients from organic sources and "seed" the lawn with microorganisms that break down thatch and encourage healthy lawn soil. To minimize excessive growth of my lawn, I fertilize only once a year in the early fall, using a formulation made for application at this time. Lawn and other cool-season grasses are in active growth at this time, and fertilization is very beneficial. Enough carries over to encourage early greenup in the spring without spurring rapid growth.

In situations requiring fertilizer, the following are recommended:

Compost We've heard it a thousand times before, but *every* garden should have a compost pile. Properly made compost in adequate quantities will provide the garden with all the good organic nutrition it needs. Compost mixed into the soil when planting annuals and vegetables or used as a mulch around permanent plants is, in the long run, the best thing for your garden and the environment. If you don't have enough material of your own, "steal" leaves from your neighbors who don't know any better and kindly bag them up and place them at curbside for pickup by municipal recycling programs (or by *your* recycling program).

Granular or water soluble chemical fertilizers are one alternative for containers and other places quickly leached of nutrients by watering. Liquid formulations tend to get to the plants quicker because they are already dissolved when applied, but granular fertilizers ultimately do the job just as well and are a little cheaper. I tend to use granular fertilizers when I first prepare the soil and plant my containers. For succeeding applications, I usually use a liquid fertilizer because it quickly gets to the roots without having to mix in with the soil and possibly cause root damage.

There is a bewildering variety of formulations on the market, each requiring different rates and frequency of application over the season. Read instructions carefully, and if in doubt, use less. It's easier to add more than to remove excess. If you suspect overfertilization, flush the container with water to leach some out. The best formulations contain, besides the standard nitrogen, phosphorus, and potassium (N, P, K), plant nutrients required in much smaller quantities, like sulfur, iron, copper, and manganese, which are analogous to vitamins for us.

Time- or slow-release fertilizers eliminate the often frustrating guesswork of using granular or liquid fertilizers, but at a higher price. These fertilizers release their nutrients slowly over the course of the growing season. Some release them based on the temperature of the soil, and others on the amount of moisture present in the soil or mix being used. Either work well, although in particularly warm areas of the country or during a hot spell where soil temperatures get too high, the temperature-release fertilizers may release too much at once. Some formulations are designed to last anywhere from 3 on up to 9 months without replenishment. I like these types of fertilizers. I use them only in my containers because of the expense, but they work very well, are easily measured out and applied, and once applied, there's no worry about hungry plants.

There are many other methods of getting fertilizer to plants, including foliar feeding with organic or chemical mixtures, root feeders, and just about any formulation you can think of, from bat guano to manure tea. You name it, and it's been done. Some may be easier to use, less expensive, or more appropriate to your area and what is being grown. All plants need nutrients. If the soil does not provide them naturally, you must help things along.

*P*runing

Grooming and pruning can be a major source of activity in the garden. Most of your annuals and perennials will benefit from your removing spent flowers or pinching them back to encourage more branching and blossoms. Early-season pinching can keep taller plants with floppy tendencies, such as Russian sage and some asters, shorter, bushier and better able to stand up without staking.

Fastidious removal of spent flowers also prevents the plants from setting seed, which takes a good deal of the plants' energy. In lieu of setting seed, a plant will put out new shoots and roots, increasing its size and overall vigor. Besides, plants look better if regularly groomed. This is a great source of hand, wrist, and arm exercise as well as hand-eye coordination. These chores are accomplished with scissors, hand pruners or long-handled pruners. The best grooming tools are your hands, if you can reach the plants. Most blooms occur on softer growth that is easily pinched off without tools.

Pruning is normally performed on dormant trees and shrubs. I believe pruning should be done only to remove dead or diseased growth, as well as crossed branches or any other misshapen growth. I prefer letting a tree or shrub take on its natural shape. However, some shrubs flower best on new growth, which is encouraged by removing older branches to make room for and stimulate new growth. Others, like the southern crape myrtle, must be regularly renewal-pruned because it flowers *only* on the current year's growth. Specialized pruning to create bonsai and topiary, or train plants against fences, walls, or trellises is also very interesting, much more labor-intensive, but fun if you have the time and skill. I prefer to select plants whose natural shape fits into my design without pruning, especially in those harder-to-get-at areas at the rear of borders.

Pruning is an art, and I refer you to the many good references on pruning and training plants. The tools of choice are long-handled loppers and saws that allow extended reach into the center of the shrub or up into the tree. On older, established, or mature trees, a certified consulting arborist will be able to perform the work safely and correctly. The best pruning jobs on trees and shrubs are "invisible" when the work is done. Do not remove too much in any one year, because leggy and disease-prone soft growth is encouraged.

Again, the degree of this work is dictated by your plant selection. You can select plants that require or benefit from regular grooming and pruning. Using your Enabling Garden as a source of exercise and activity, you may lean toward more plants that need more work. I would be disappointed if my garden was carefree. I enjoy routine grooming of plants, at least for the time being. As time goes on, this may change with my abilities, and by reworking the planting or structural design of my Enabling Garden, I'll keep it as enabling as I wish.

*P*est and Disease Control

The specific insects and diseases that are going to affect your garden are dictated by your location, the plants you grow, and any seasonal variation that may enhance a particular problem in your area or one that can be cyclical or worse in one year than the next. You need to seek local information to know what problems are prevalent in your area and what treatments are recommended. Your local Cooperative Extension Service and public garden, coupled with your and your neighbors' lifetimes of experience, should be able to correct any problems you may have.

The key is to know exactly what you are dealing with, controlling it with the least toxic methods first, rather than immediately resorting to general toxic warfare, and *being safe*. In the Enabling Garden, this is particularly important because most chemical controls are poisons of widely varying toxicity to humans. Perhaps a chemical also has only a very specific, narrow range of pests for which it is effective. These poisons will affect some of us more than others if we come in contact with the chemical itself or the treated plants, particularly if we are taking medications, which may interact negatively with the chemical. Contact with any pesticides at all could be dangerous. You may have allergic reactions as well, so it's best when using chemical controls to check with your doctor regarding any restrictions. We all know a bee sting, a painful but harmless encounter for most of us, can be deadly for someone with a specific allergic intolerance.

The best way to avoid accidental reactions or poisonings in your Enabling Garden is to minimize chemical use in the first place. This can be done by implementing what is called Integrated Pest Management, a program of pest control that relies on a combination of least toxic, biological, cultural, and mechanical controls to target a specific pest, preferably at the most vulnerable point in its life cycle or anytime the problem occurs.

Prior to this however, a pest and disease control program can be enhanced by these strategies.

⊛ Avoid plants that are prone to problems in the first place. For example, here in Chicago most roses are affected by aphids, powdery mildew, and black spot. Unless treated regularly to avoid these problems, roses quickly decline. Most *rugosa* and many other shrub roses are perfectly fine. Avoid plants that need poison, rather than poison the garden.

⊛ Select plants with built-in disease or insect resistance. Many plants native to your area have adapted to local problems and are therefore less susceptible, or at least more tolerant. Many vegetables and other plants have been bred or selected specifically for resistance to pest and disease problems, such as "VFNT" tomatoes. Seek out lists of such plants for your area.

⊛ Use proper plant cultural methods to keep plants healthy and hence more resistant to pests and diseases. Avoid conditions that may promote a problem, such as working in the garden when leaves are wet or watering foliage late in the day, which encourages fungal diseases to grow and spread during lengthy humid and wet periods.

⊛ Tolerate a few bugs or blemishes without running for the sprayer. Organic gardeners have learned this. What does it matter if the outer layer of the cabbage leaves has a few holes in it, as long as the cabbage is okay? Learn to tolerate a certain level of damage as being part of nature. Rarely do you see the totally unblemished plant by the end of the season. Most plants can tolerate a nibble or two without harm.

⊛ Always! Always! Always!—**no matter what method you use—follow directions, wear appropriate clothing, and use any other equipment called for, such as rubber gloves and eye protection. Cut absolutely no corners in this area!**

A program of Integrated Pest Management is accurate in insect, weed, or disease identification, then utilizes the least toxic methods, up to and including chemicals, if necessary as the only useful control. *You* are part of the least toxic methods. Hand-picking easily seen tomato hornworms off a couple of tomato plants is better than *any* chemical, even if it's totally safe. A few caterpillars on a maple tree may turn out to be an unusual moth native to your area but rarely seen. Know this before running for the Bacillis Thuringiensis (BT), one of the best killers of the butterfly and moth families and reputed to be harmless to humans. (However, recently cases have been reported of both increased resistance by some insects and a few allergic reactions in humans—just to make the point that *you never know!*)

Other nontoxic methods may include special devices to either attract beneficial or predacious insects to your yard or trap the nasty ones altogether. With the latter, however, you run the risk of attracting more pests to your yard than would normally be there in the first place. Using sticky traps of a color attractive to the targeted insect, releasing lady bugs, placing out a few purchased praying mantis egg cases in the spring, or any other manner of biological pest control on the market is effective and fun to try. Low-toxicity chemical controls that prevent seed germination can be used for weed control in the lawn, and there are formulations for use in ornamental beds, as well. They must be used before seeds germinate to be effective. These certainly offer an alternative to later hand-weeding or increasingly toxic methods.

Various fungal and bacterial diseases are more difficult to positively identify and may be masked by environmental damage. Controls would be totally ineffective for such problems as browning leaf tips, caused by drought in the spring, while young leaves were unfurling—not a fungal disease. Where disease is correctly identified, though, sprays should be targeted to the proper disease and at the best time of the season to maximize effectiveness with a minimal number of applications and strengths. Usually, by the time you see symptoms of some fungal diseases, sprays are ineffective. You must know when spores are active and target applications at these times.

This is all somewhat complicated, but worthwhile if we are going to protect the environment and not create toxic waste dumps in our own yards. I generally work organically whenever I can and minimize chemical use of any kind, but there are a few problems on large trees in my yard, problems that I inherited with the house, which would destroy them without protection. For those and spot-weeding in my lawn, I use chemical controls. Once you gain some experience in your own yard, you will begin to know the typical problems you encounter there. You can then devise your own program of controls and won't have to continually search out information on the best and least toxic methods to use. Just don't use an indiscriminate or routine program against problems you may not have.

Proper plant selection, tolerance of a little damage, and a well-planned program of integrated pest management will minimize pest and disease problems in the first place, protect our environment, and protect you from unnecessary exposure to potentially harmful chemical controls.

*F*all Maintenance

The first real killing frosts of fall are the signal to put the Enabling Garden to rest for the winter. Fall, after the leaves drop, is a good time to plant trees and shrubs. Cut back perennials to a few inches above the ground. Exceptions are ornamental grasses and others, like purple coneflowers, *Rudbeckia*, or some sedums, that lend color and form to your winter landscape in their foliage, seedpods, and flower heads. These should be cut back *before* new growth begins in the spring. You can leave smaller garden debris in place to serve as mulch and ultimately decay. Add the balance to the new compost pile—hopefully, the old one had been used up during the season.

Fallen leaves are usually left in place in my ornamental beds. Those collected from the lawn are also added to next year's compost pile. This is also the time to "steal" leaves from your neighbors as well, if you can use them and they don't mind. All leaves are best shredded or run over with the lawnmower as they will have less tendency to blow around, and this concentrates their nutrients into smaller volumes as well. Shredded leaves and other landscape debris can be applied as a mulch to trees and shrubs in autumn, but wait till the ground freezes before applying winter mulch to perennials and other tender plants. Applying mulch before this time may keep the plants from becoming fully dormant before the onset of real cold weather, which would damage the plants if they're not dormant.

Dead annuals and debris from the vegetable garden should be removed from ground-level areas, raised beds, and other containers and added to the compost pile. The last of this year's compost or a few leaves can be roughly tilled into barren vegetable and annual flower areas, with a final 2- to 3-inch layer of organic matter over the top to prevent exposed soil from eroding and to keep the underlying soil from freezing as long as possible. This encourages more rapid decomposition of the newly added organic matter. You would be surprised how late in the fall and how early in the spring how many earthworms and decomposing insects are active, if you pull back this mulch layer for a look.

Empty all pots, window boxes, and other small containers into the compost pile. You should add fresh soil to all small containers every year. Also, replace soilless mixes every year. Any large clay pots and other containers that would be damaged by winter freeze-thaw action should be emptied, at least partially. Otherwise, move and store them where they have a chance to dry out before the soil in them freezes, expands, and breaks the expensive containers. Water in cracks will also tend to break containers when frozen. Covering containers with large trash bags, tied down with rope or elastic cords, will also work, if the soil has dried somewhat first.

All wooden structures should be inspected for loosening screws or other joints. File or sand away rough areas that would cause slivers, and apply wood sealers or other preservatives, carefully following manufacturers' directions for amounts and frequency. There are newer, water-based preservatives on the market that I feel are worth a try, as they are better for the environment. You can often tell it's fall, with the smell of paint and wood preservatives in the air. This is also when paint and other needed materials are usually on sale.

This is also the time to clean, sharpen, and oil your tools. Again, sand any rough wooden handles. Some gardeners keep a pail of sand with old crankcase oil in it for dipping their tools after each use. With a can of spray lubricant and rust inhibitor, I thoroughly coat all metal surfaces before I put them away for the winter. Remove any materials that should not freeze from outdoor storage areas. Disconnect and store hoses and other watering equipment, too.

This is also the time I make some notes on what plants I want to move in the spring, what's starting to get out of bounds, and what has or hasn't worked. Note empty spots where a few new plants can be squeezed in, so you can look forward to the catalogs and spring plant sales. These last journal entries are very helpful for next year's garden.

Spring Maintenance

Spring maintenance should be very easy if you finished everything on the fall list. A few routine checks will get your garden off to the right start. Inspect wooden containers and structures again for potential slivers, loosened screws, and other mystifying damage that may have occurred over winter.

Paving may have cracked from frost heaving or settling; they should be repaired if a tripping hazard has been created. Loosened pavers should be reset. Gravel surfaces may need to be recompacted where freezing and thawing has loosened them. It should be noted that properly installed surfaces will not have these problems, which are generally caused by improper drainage and base preparation.

Large containers and raised beds, which are filled with our highly organic soil mix, may need to be topped off with fresh soil as the organic matter decomposes and settling occurs. The small containers we emptied in the fall must be positioned for planting and refilled with fresh soilless mix. Beyond a quick sweep of the patio, hooking up the hoses, and positioning your favorite lawn chair, you're ready to go for another exciting season in the Enabling Garden.

A Last Word

I have said this before, but it deserves mentioning again: Don't be afraid to ask for help or hire out the chores that are physically too hard for you. There is always someone who is willing to help. I hire to have my lawn cut, annuals and vegetable beds turned over in the spring, trees pruned, and mulch spread over my large beds. Most of the rest I can handle, but that will probably change with time, and I'll have to redesign or adapt to those new challenges, as we do with everything else.

I have tried to show you throughout this book that you can design your garden to suit any need or ability. Maintenance can be as easy or as challenging as you wish. Just don't quit, because, hopefully, I have shown you many ideas that *enable* you to keep going. Those of us with mobility impairments know our lives are a constant series of adaptations, and we succeed—we're masters at it. We gain a greater appreciation for the beauty of the little things that make life worthwhile. For me and millions of others, the garden offers many of those things, certainly not all of them, but my life and the lives of those millions of others would be less complete without our gardens, big or small. What we've tapped into in our gardens is not often easily explained or rationalized, but those of us who garden know that we benefit from the experience. No one should either miss out on the experience or have to stop.

Sources of Help

The following lists offer places where you can seek help. Some of the books may be out of print and must be sought out at the library. As I mentioned previously, many sources of equipment come and go, so these lists should not be considered static. In regard to plant references, I have listed those which have been very useful to me over the years and are applicable to wide areas of the country. (*Addresses and telephone numbers were current at the time of publication but are subject to change.*)

*P*ublic Enabling Gardens

At this time there are a few public Enabling Garden demonstrations where you can see many of the innovations described in this book. There are many others planned at public gardens throughout the country that will be publicized as they are completed. Hundreds of others are located on private property or at medical institutions where horticultural therapy programs are located. Many of these will welcome you, but you should contact them first. You can find those nearest you by contacting the American or Canadian Horticultural Therapy Associations mentioned later.

Chicago Botanic Garden
Enabling Garden for People with Disabilities
Horticultural Therapy Services
P.O. Box 400
Glencoe, Illinois 60022
(708) 835-8248

Denver Botanic Garden
Morrison Horticultural Demonstration Center
909 York Street
Denver, Colorado 80206
(303) 370-8040

Enid A. Haupt Glass Garden
The Howard A. Rusk Institute of Rehabilitation Medicine
400 East 34th Street
New York, New York 10016
(212) 263-6058

The Minnesota Landscape Arboretum
Clotilde Irvine Sensory Garden and Therapeutic Horticulture Program Center
3675 Arboretum Drive
Chanhassen, Minnesota 55317-0039
(612) 443-2460

Sea World of Ohio
Access for All Garden
1100 Sea World Drive
Aurora, Ohio 44202-8706
(800) 637-4268

Organizations

American Horticultural Therapy Association
326A Christopher Avenue
Gaithersburg, Maryland 20879
(800) 634-1603
(Monthly newsletter, journal, membership directory, network of regional chapters, annual conference)

The American Horticultural Therapy Association (AHTA) is the sole national organization in the United States concerned with the promotion and development of horticultural therapy and rehabilitation programs. AHTA is dedicated to the development of horticultural therapy efforts which serve and train disabled and disadvantaged persons. The AHTA is also vitally concerned with the professional development, education, and enhanced expertise of horticultural therapy practitioners. Horticultural therapy is gaining national recognition and acceptance because of the efforts of the AHTA.

Other excellent sources for ideas and help are the many organizations—such as hospitals, rehabilitation facilities, nursing homes, retirement communities, and nationwide groups that direct services to people with disabilities and older adults—that have established horticultural therapy programs and employ horticultural therapists.

American Community Gardening Association
325 Walnut Street
Philadelphia, Pennsylvania 19106
(215) 625-8280
(Journal, newsletter, annual conference)

American Foundation for the Blind
15 West 16th Street
New York, New York 10011
(212) 620–2000 (voice)
(212) 620–2158 (text telephone)

Provides information on assistive technology, job accommodations, and products. Evaluates assistive technologies.

American Printing House for the Blind
1839 Frankfort Avenue
Louisville, Kentucky 40206
(502) 895–2405 (voice only)

Braille publisher. Also distributes material in large print and audio recordings. Provides instructional aids, computer software, and textbooks for children.

Apple Computer—Worldwide Disability Solutions Group
20525 Mariani Avenue
Cupertino, California 95014
(408) 974–7910 (voice only)

Program and resource referral, data base on accommodations produced by Apple and others. Publishes consumer booklets, videotapes.

Barrier Free Environments Inc.
P.O. Box 30634
Raleigh, North Carolina 27622
(919) 782–7823

Consultation and publications firm on general accessible design.

Canadian Horticultural Therapy Association
c/o Royal Botanic Gardens
P.O. Box 399
Hamilton, Ontario, Canada L8N 3H8
(Quarterly newsletter)

Horticultural Therapy
Goulds Ground
Vallis Way
Frome, Somerset
England BA1130W

Publishes quarterly *Growth Point* magazine, packed full of barrier-free gardening ideas and experiences. Other publications available.

IBM National Support Center for Persons with Disabilities
P.O. Box 2150
Atlanta, Georgia 30301
(800) 426–4832
(800) 426–3388

Has extensive data base on adaptive technology, publishes resource guides organized by disability, and offers training programs in computer skills for people with disabilities.

National Council on Independent Living
Troy Atrium
4th Street and Broadway
Troy, New York 12180
(518) 274-1979

Contact this organization for the local independent living center near you. Great source of support and technical assistance.

National Gardening Association
180 Flynn Avenue
Burlington, Vermont 05401
(Magazine, other publications)

North American Fruit Explorers
Rt. 1, Box 94
Chapin, Illinois 62628
(217) 245–7589

Essential source of information on dwarf fruit trees, antique varieties, and some of the best-flavored fruits not found in stores. There are also dozens of other specialty plant societies elsewhere, offering information and assistance with their specialties, from begonias to roses.

Whole Access
517 Lincoln Avenue
Redwood City, California 94061
(415) 363–2647 (voice or text telephone)

Focused on training to professionals. Dedicated to every person's needs to experience nature and outdoor recreation. Provides workshops, access surveys, consultation, and public education.

❁

*A*daptive Gardening and Independent Living

Beems, J. (1986). *Adaptive Gardening Equipment: A Resource Manual for Patients, Families, and Professionals.* (Available from Craig Hospital, 3425 South Clarkston, Englewood, Colorado 80110.) Basic guide to tools, raised beds, and more.

Burke, K. (Ed.) (1983). *Gardening in Containers.* San Francisco: Ortho Books. This and any other book on container gardening will be a source of useful ideas for raising the soil to a comfortable height.

Chaplin, M. (1978). *Gardening with the Physically Handicapped and Elderly.* London: B.T. Batsford.

Hale, G. (Ed.) (1979). *The Source Book for the Disabled: An Illustrated Guide to Easier and More Independent Living for Physically Disabled People, Their Families and Friends.* New York: Paddington Press.

Lunt, S. (1982). *Handbook for the Disabled: Ideas and Inventions for Easier Living.* New York: Charles Scribner's Sons.

Moore, B. (1989). *Growing with Gardening: A Horticultural Therapy Training Manual.* Chapel Hill, North Carolina: University of North Carolina Press. An excellent guide to adapting activities in the garden.

Ocone, L. & Thabault, G. (Eds.) (1984). *Tools and Techniques for Easier Gardening.* Burlington, Vermont: Gardens for All. This booklet, now out of print, was one of the first of its kind to deal with barrier-free gardening. I consulted on this project. The booklet is very good but, unfortunately, hard to find. It primarily discusses tools and structures. The organization is now called the National Gardening Association. See organization section.

Olwell, C. (1990). *Gardening from the Heart—Why Gardeners Garden.* Berkeley, California: Antelope Island Press.

Relf, P.D. (1987). *Gardening in Raised Beds and Containers for the Elderly and Physically Handicapped.* Blacksburg, Virginia: Virginia Polytechnic Institute and State University.

Restuccio, J.P. (1992). *Fitness the Dynamic Gardening Way: A Health and Wellness Lifestyle.* Cordova, Tennessee: Balance of Nature Publishing. An interesting book that uses gardening for exercise, weight loss, and an overall wellness lifestyle. Useful when planning or gearing activity for those with mobility impairments.

Rothert, E. & Daubert, J. (1981). *Horticultural Therapy at a Physical Rehabilitation Facility.* Glencoe, Illinois: Chicago Horticultural Society.

Rothert, E. & Daubert, J. (1981). *Horticultural Therapy for Nursing Homes, Senior Centers and Retirement Living.* Glencoe, Illinois: Chicago Horticultural Society.

Schweller, F.J. (1989). *Container Gardening for the Handicapped.* (Available from Hand-D-Cap Publishing, 1027 East Las Palmaritas Drive, Phoenix, Arizona 85020). Employs a very inexpensive cinder block and plank system to create shelves upon which containers are placed within easy reach. Great for temporary needs.

The Wheelabout Garden. (1980). (Available from the National Easter Seal Society, 2023 West Ogden Avenue, Chicago, Illinois 60612).

White, A.S., Nicholas, P.J.R., Hay, R., Bach, F., Chaplin M., Tyldesley B., & Elliott, P.H. (1972). *The Easy Path to Gardening.* London: Reader's Digest Association. One of the first books of its kind available in this country. Very useful barrier-free structures and design ideas.

Magazines

Accent on Living
P.O. Box 700
Bloomington, IL 61702

Quarterly magazine on independent living, new equipment, and more.

Access USA News
P.O. Box 1134
Crystal Lake, IL 60039

Arthritis Today
1314 Spring Street NW
Atlanta, GA 30309-2898

Mainstream
2973 Beech Street
San Diego, CA 92102

Modern Maturity
3200 Carson Street
Lakewood, CA 90712-4038

General Gardening References

Bartholomew, M. (1981). *Square Foot Gardening*. Emmaus, Pennsylvania: Rodale Press. Excellent intensive-gardening book. Particularly useful for the blind or visually impaired gardener because the garden layout is in a grid pattern.

Bradley, F. (Ed.). *Rodale's Chemical Free Yard and Garden*. Emmaus, Pennsylvania: Rodale Press.

Burke, K. (Ed.). (1981). *All About Annuals*. San Francisco, California: Ortho Books.

Burke, K. (1982). *Easy Maintenance Gardening*. San Francisco, California: Ortho Books.

Carr, A. (1979). *Rodale's Color Handbook of Garden Insects*. Emmaus, Pennsylvania: Rodale Press.

Clausen, R.R. & Ekstrom, N.H. (1989). *Perennials for American Gardens*. New York: Random House. One of the more comprehensive books on perennial plants, complete with color illustrations, sources, common and Latin name indexes, and lists of various perennial plant societies.

Crockett, J.U. (1981). *Crockett's Flower Garden*. Boston: Little, Brown.

Crockett, J.U. (1979). *Crockett's Tool Shed*. Boston: Little, Brown. An excellent primer on garden tools.

Crockett, J.U. (1977). *Crockett's Victory Garden*. Boston: Little, Brown.

Dirr, M.A. (1983). *Manual of Woody Landscape Plants*, 4th ed. Champaign, Illinois: Stipes. One of the best for evaluating trees and shrubs for your yard. Has line drawings but lacks photographs.

Dirr, M.A. (1990). *Photographic Manual of Woody Landscape Plants*. Champaign, Illinois: Stipes. Companion to the previous, with black-and-white photographs.

Fell, D. (1983). *Annuals, How to Select, Grow and Enjoy*. Los Angeles: Price/Stern/Sloan.

The Garden Expert Series (various authors and publication dates). England: Jarold and Sons. One of the better inexpensive references, with volumes on flowers, trees and shrubs, bedding plants, roses, lawns, vegetables, fruits, and so on.

Gardening Shortcuts. (1976). San Francisco: Ortho Books.

Hill, L. (1979). *Pruning Simplified*. Emmaus, Pennsylvania: Rodale Press.

Holton, A. (1986). *All about Bulbs*. San Francisco: Ortho Books.

Kowalchik, C. & Hylton, W. (Eds.). *Rodale's Illustrated Encyclopedia of Herbs*. Emmaus, Pennsylvania: Rodale Press.

Lampe, Dr. F. & McCann, M. (1985). *AMA Handbook of Poisonous and Injurious Plants*. Chicago: American Medical Association.

National Gardening Association (Eds). (1986). *Gardening: The Complete Guide to Growing America's Favorite Fruits and Vegetables*. Reading, Pennsylvania: Addison-Wesley.

Ottesen, C. (1989). *Ornamental Grasses—The Amber Wave*. New York: McGraw Hill.

Sinnes, A. (1979). *All About Fertilizers, Soils and Water*. San Francisco: Ortho Books.

Thomson, B. (1987). *The New Victory Garden*. Boston: Little, Brown.

The Time-Life Series of Gardening (various authors and publication dates). This over-20-volume set contains easy-to-follow instruction and detailed plant lists.

Wyman, D. (1977). *Wyman's Gardening Encyclopedia*. New York: Macmillan. A recently revised, excellent gardening reference.

Magazines

Fine Gardening
The Taunton Press
63 South Main Street
P.O. Box 5506
Newton, Connecticut 06470

Flower and Garden
KC Publishing
700 West 47th Street, Suite 310
Kansas City, Missouri 64112

National Gardening
National Gardening Association
180 Flynn Avenue
Burlington, Vermont 05401

Organic Gardening
Rodale Press
33 East Minor Street
Emmaus, Pennsylvania 18098

Landscape Design and Construction

These are general design references, not specifically covering enabling gardens. Most take you through step-by-step processes resulting in the final plan. Many include good advice on how to build the garden, as well.

Atkinson, S. (1990). *Sunset: The Complete Patio Book*. Menlo Park, California: Lane.

Brooks, J. (1991). *The Book of Garden Design*. New York: Macmillan. Lavishly illustrated, with thousands of ideas, good step-by-step instructions.

Brooks, J. (1978). *The Small Garden*. New York: Macmillan. Superb reference for designing smaller properties. Lots of paving ideas. Hundreds of excellent ideas, and many design examples illustrated.

Cotton, L., ASLA. (1980). *All About Landscaping*. San Francisco: Ortho Books. Easy to follow, inexpensive.

Cox, J. (1991). *Landscaping with Nature*. Emmaus, Pennsylvania: Rodale Press.

Creasy, R. (1982). *The Complete Book of Edible Landscaping*. San Francisco: Sierra Club Books.

Feller-Roth, B. (1989). *Landscape Plans*. San Francisco: Ortho Books. Good source of ideas.

Giles, F. (1986). *Landscape Construction Procedures, Techniques and Design*. Champaign, Illinois: Stipes.

Hayward, G. (1993). *Garden Paths—Inspiring Designs and Practical Products*. Charlotte, Vermont: Camden House.

Hessayon, Dr. D.G. (1992). *The Garden Do-It-Yourself Expert*. England: Jarrold and Sons. A small, inexpensive guide on building all the nonliving things in the garden. The entire Expert Series is excellent, inexpensive, and easily understood.

Hogan, E. (Ed.). (1972). *Sunset: Ideas for Landscaping*. Menlo Park, California: Lane. Inexpensive, easy to follow.

Klein R. (Ed.). (1975). *How to Build Walks, Walls and Patio Floors*. Menlo Park, California: Lane.

Krause, D. *Designing Barrier Free Areas*. (Available from New York State College of Agriculture and Life Services, Instructional Materials Service, Cornell University, Ithaca, New York 14853).

Nelson, W.R., Jr. (1975). *Landscaping Your Home*. Urbana-Champaign, Illinois: University of Illinois Cooperative Extension Service. Circular IIII.

Rider, K. (1987). *Wood Projects for the Garden*. San Francisco: Ortho Books.

Smith, L. (1976). *Do It Yourself Garden Construction Know How*. San Francisco: Ortho Books.

Wirth, T. (1984). *The Victory Garden Landscape Guide*. Boston: Little, Brown.

Magazines

Garden Design
4401 Connecticut Avenue, NW, Suite 500
Washington, D.C. 20008

Landscape Architecture
American Society of Landscape Architects
4401 Connecticut Avenue, NW, 5th floor
Washington, D.C. 20008
(800) 787-LAMS

Both the above are excellent references for design and material ideas, suppliers of materials, and local associations that can put you in touch with licensed landscape architects. Latter offers a publications list, some on designing outdoor areas for people with disabilities and older adults.

Paving Ideas and Materials

Bomanite Corporation
(800) 854–2094
Dyed and textured concrete.

The Concrete Paver Institute
Division of National Concrete Masonry Association
2302 Horse Pen Road
Herndon, Virginia 22071
(703) 713-1900

Not-for-profit organization promoting the manufacturers, contractors, and products of the industry.

Saf-Dek
No Fault Industries
11325 Pennywood Avenue
Baton Rouge, Louisiana 70809
(800) 232–7766

A seamless, porous resilient, granular, rubber safety surface made from recycled rubber. Typically used around swimming pools and children's play lots.

Containers

The Easy Gardener Company Limited
Oaklands, West Street Lane
Maynards Green, Heathfield
East Sussex TN21 ODB
(04353) 3634 TEL
(04353) 3542 FAX

Uses a tabletop format to raise soil; various
models and configurations are offered. Shipping to
this country is expensive, but their catalog may spur
ideas. One of the few companies manufacturing garden containers specifically for people with limited
mobility.

Local bakery
(5-gallon plastic pails)

Local construction supply company
(Flue tiles, sewer pipes)

OS Plastic, Inc.
3091 Holcomb Bridge Road
Suite M2
Norcross, Georgia 30071
(404) 448–7701

Poly Planters
P.O. Box 3504
Thousand Oaks, California 91359
(805) 525–8800
(800) 322–3112

Rubbermaid Specialty Products, Inc.
3330 Taylorsville Road
Statesville, North Carolina 28677
(704) 878–9551

Terracast
4700 Mitchell Street
North Las Vegas, Nevada 89031
(800) 423–8539

Valley View Specialties
Venus Polyspun Planters
13834 South Kortner
Crestwood, Illinois 60445
(312) 597–0885
(800) 323–9369

Tools and Equipment

Most of the following are catalog companies, which
makes it difficult to try a tool before purchase, although many do have return privileges. The same
products may be available from several companies.
No endorsement is intended.

Adaptability
P.O. Box 515
Colchester, Connecticut 06415
(800) 243–9232

Loaded with products for independent living,
with many applications to home and garden.

Alsto's Handy Helpers
P.O. Box 1267
Galesburg, Illinois 61401
(800) 447–0048

One of the better selections of handy outdoor
equipment, including cordless tools, furniture, long-
handled tools, hand tools, loppers, trellises, and
ready-made raised beds and containers that incorporate seating.

American Intertool, Inc.
1255 Tonne Road
Elk Grove Village, Illinois 60007
(800) 334–3675

One source for my favorite long-handled pruners made by ARS Tool Company, with interchangeable heads and multilength handles and extensions.

American Standard Company
P.O. Box 325
Plantsville, Connecticut 06479
(203) 628–9643
General tools, some lightweight; excellent
  shears.

Ames Lawn and Garden Tools
Box 1774
3801 Camdell Avenue
Parkersburg, West Virginia 26101
(800) 624–2654

General garden tools: good long-handled, lightweight, smaller bladed spades, cultivators, hoes,
and more.

Brookstone Company
1655 Bassford Drive
Mexico, Missouri 65265
(314) 581-7113
Many useful items for the gardener.

Clapper's Garden Catalog
1121 Washington Street
West Newton, Massachusetts 02165
(617) 244-7909
Top-quality tools and other garden equipment.

Enrichments
P.O. Box 471
Western Spring, Illinois 60558
(800) 323-5547

An excellent selection of products, tools, and equipment for independent life, including reachers, gripping aids, lap boards or trays, and lower back supports.

Gardener's Eden
P.O. Box 7307
San Francisco, California 94120
(415) 421-7900
Some useful tools for older gardeners.

Gardener's Supply Company
128 Intervale Road
Burlington, Vermont 05401
(802) 863-1700

One of the better suppliers of lightweight, small-bladed, long- and short-handled tools, long-handled seeders, small power tillers, scissors, loppers, easy kneeler, knee pads, and other useful enabling devices.

Good Idea
P.O. Box 955
Vail, Colorado 81658
(800) 538-6690

General handy-items catalog, with some enabling tools and equipment for the garden.

Habilus—Ergonomic Products for Capability
Box 2265 Square One
100 City Centre Drive
Mississauga, Ontario
Canada L5R 3C8
(905) 712-0237

Mail-order firm with several types of excellent self-opening scissors and pruners, ergonomically designed knives, Easy Wheeler wheelbarrow, and Easy Gripper.

Lever-Aide Garden Tools
1357 Park Road, Dept. CBG
Chanhassen, Minnesota 55317

A set of three hand tools designed for greater efficiency, less fatigue, and require little gripping power.

Walter Nicke
P.O. Box 433
36 McLeod Lane
Topsfield, Massachusetts 01983
(508) 887-3338

A good selection of enabling tools and equipment at reasonable prices.

Radio Flyer, Inc.
6515 Grand Avenue
Chicago, Illinois 60635
(312) 637-7100

Wheelbarrows, carts, and wagons we knew as kids.

Smith and Hawken
25 Corte Madera
Mill Valley, California 94941
(415) 383-4415

Containers, tools, clothing, furniture, and some special enabling tools.

Florist Products
2242 North Palmer Drive
Schaumburg, Illinois 60173
(708) 885-2242

A.H. Hummert Seed Co.
2746 Chouteau Avenue
St. Louis, Missouri 63103
(314) 771-0646

A. M. Leonard, Inc.
241 Fox Drive
Piqua, Ohio 45356
(513) 773-2694

The above three companies are professional horticultural suppliers with general merchandise.

No enabling tool sections, their catalogs illustrate a wide range of tools and equipment which could be adapted.

> J.A. Preston Corporation
> P.O. Box 89
> Jackson, Michigan 49204
> (800) 631–7277

> The Illustrated Directory of Handicapped
>   Products
> 3600 Timber Court
> Lawrence, Kansas 66049

Both are major catalog companies that sell equipment for physical therapy and rehabilitation. As such, they offer a wide range of equipment for independent living, items like foam padding for tool handles, wheelchair equipment, lap trays, reachers—you name it. I always get a couple of ideas for the garden when I page through one of these catalogs.

Index